Affiliate Marketing

How to Make Money & Create an Income

Andy Anderson

Table of Contents

Andy Anderson

Introduction

Congratulations on purchasing Affiliate Marketing: How to Make Money & Create an Income!

Affiliate marketing is a phrase you often come across online. There are literally thousands of articles telling you why you should be raking in the dollars with affiliate marketing, and you can feel a bit left out of the loop if your PayPal account isn't clocking up cash while you sleep.

But what exactly is affiliate marketing, and how can you harness its power to make money online and create a perpetual stream of passive income? Put simply, affiliate marketing is what you do when you promote or sell somebody else's product or service. You then earn a commission on any sales, or clicks through to the affiliate website. Doesn't that sound absolutely delightful?

In theory, you could have a website with no products or services of your own – maybe a blog, online journal or 'how to' or hobby site. As long as it has some connection with the product or service you are good to go. Clearly, your website costs money to maintain, and one way to cover that is to partner with affiliates to promote their products and services, especially if those products and services are linked to your particular niche.

Affiliate marketing is good for the website owner and the business concerned, because the webmaster gets a chance to earn some cash to keep the site going, and the business associate reaches a wider audience with his products and services. This double advantage model is what makes the affiliate marketing concept a hit. The really good thing about all this is that nobody loses and everybody gains. It doesn't cost the Webmaster anything to sign up to an affiliate program, and the business owner doesn't pay out until he makes the sale. Since that sale is to a customer outside of his normal promotional reach, it's a bonus. So it is a win- win situation for both parties and something that helps both in making the most of their time and effort.

So, affiliate marketing is mutually beneficial, but who can benefit from it and how do you get into it? More importantly, how can you make money from it online, and create an ongoing passive income stream? This book will tell you how.

There are separate chapters dedicated to exploring the individual aspects of this topic and something that will allow you to understand how affiliate marketing works. Once you have an idea of how it operates, you will have the chance to start affiliate marketing and use it to earn a parallel source of income that you can use to supplement your regular income.

I hope you enjoy reading this book and I thank you for choosing it.

Let us begin.

Andy Anderson

Chapter 1
What Is Affiliate Marketing?

Selling a product can be hard if you are not able to reach out to your target audience. You would sometimes end up needing to go to other means in order to sell your product. On the other hand, you may not be able to earn the money that you need for your everyday life. It is possible that you need to earn more than what you are currently earning to provide not only for yourself but also for your family as well. It may also be because you want to be able to earn money for your own gain. In cases like these, both parties can take advantage of going with affiliate marketing.

Affiliate marketing, in simple terms, is when a "vendor" is able to sell their products with the help of an "affiliate." The affiliate will be the one who markets the products to potential customers, allowing the vendor to have a sale, and in turn, they will pay the affiliate for the effort that they are able to put into selling.

PC Flowers created the concept for affiliate marketing & Gifts founder William J. Tobin. It was with a partnership with the Prodigy Network that they were able to sell, and they were able to pay Prodigy Network for their services.

You wouldn't really realize it, but all around, affiliate marketing is happening. The simplest form can be with reviews of products and services posted through the media like newspapers, magazines, television and the Internet. Using the Internet for affiliate marketing is also a common ground now, with advertisements posted in websites, and when searching for items, certain hits can be created with a search engine and it can show the item that is being sold.

Companies like Amazon have been able to establish its own affiliate marketing program, and Amazon's has been ongoing ever since July 1996. Amazon would have banners bearing their name in their affiliates' websites, and when a customer would click on those, they will be redirected to the Amazon website, and the affiliate will be paid for that service.

This is a common practice nowadays, and it is also an easy way for someone to earn money, once everything is done right.

Chapter 2
History of Affiliate Marketing

Affiliate marketing is quite popular form of digital marketing. And this is a performance based form of marketing wherein the retailers commission or compensation received for the services provided would depend upon the number of customers they can acquire due to the influence exuberated in the form of marketing efforts. Think of affiliate marketing as a reward. So it generally can be understood as a reward based program depending upon the sales. In the present world it has become quite popular, but how exactly did this practice come into being?

Before the Internet also the term affiliate marketing exited. Though not many are aware of this fact since it is a preconceived notion that it has always been used according to the online context. But it is true that this concept has been around since before the advent of the Internet. But even till this date, this concept of affiliate marketing exists even offline. Don't believe me? Well how many of you have got a discount at your hairdresser when you referred a friend? I am sure a lot of you did, so this indeed is an example of the extremely popular concept of affiliate marketing. But this marketing gimmick wasn't as widespread as it is now because before the use of the World Wide Web, this technique proved to have a few too many hurdles. Because, it is essential for the monetary payment in this technique, to be able to track the referral code and in the olden days that wasn't quite possible.

The Internet revolution pretty much changed the way we lead our lives. The Internet revolution wasn't confined to only one aspect, everything and anything was changed and advertising was no exception. Internet proved to be the holy grail of information. People began trusting the Internet for any information they required. They started looking at it for reviews of products, information and even recommendations. The Web became an indispensable part of an individual's life. So it is not a surprise that even the field of advertisements was revolutionized. There came a need to change the strategies of advertising. The number of technological developments kept on increasing. It didn't look like the Internet was a phenomenon that had to be taken easily.

It was here to stay and it still it. With the introduction of cookies and Web 2.0, these made the possibility of tracking the impact advertisement had on the aspect of buying. To track the impact the Internet had on customers. Now to this, let us add the Internet explosion in the form of ecommerce in late 90'S and the advent of blogs in early 2000 and the tech savvy generation that was to follow. All these things paved the way for the introduction of affiliate marketing.

The very first program for affiliate marketing was the brainchild of William Tobin and he implemented this. Not just that, he even patented it. He, as we know it today conceived the concept of affiliate marketing, and he also set up the first affiliate program for his company in the year 1989. That's how affiliate marketing came into being.

The second company that took up affiliate marketing is Amazon. The ecommerce giant used affiliate marketing in the year 1996 launch one of its associated programs. This indeed is considered to be a milestone in the history of affiliate marketing, because it totally perceived the way in which people and industry perceived affiliate marketing. And this attracted global interest and even retailers wanted to find a way in which they could implement it for themselves. And after this there was no turning back.

In the year 1998, the first set of affiliate networks was launched. And the two things launched were the commission junction and the clickbank. For online retailers, this proved to be quite a helpful innovation. Because it made affiliate marketing a lot more easy and accessible for smaller retailers and it also offered payment solutions and exchange between merchants was also facilitated in an easier manner. In the year 2000, the Unite States Federal Trade Commission, that controlled trade regulation in USA, provided guidelines for this sector. And this provided the required validation to build for the legitimacy and validity of affiliate marketing in the world of marketing.

By the year 2012 in the United Kingdom, affiliate marketing represented a little over 6% of the entire nation's online economy and a little over £9 billion in the form of sales according to the statistics published. Affiliate marketing is a field with immense potential and with the online stores trying to best each other; the scope of it is ever increasing. Affiliate marketing is not just confined to the western and European nations, but even the Asian market has made a place for itself in the global market.

Chapter 3

What Are The Benefits Of Affiliate Marketing?

Affiliate marketing complements and there are cases where it replaces other offline and online marketing strategies as a very important channel for marketing. In affiliate marketing, anyone do not need to invest any time and effort in creating a product or service to sell, once you have a platform to sell a product or service, you can start selling those products or services already.

Companies and individuals can utilize the power of affiliate marketing to help them earn profit from each sale they are making. Other than these, here are the other benefits of affiliate marketing:

1. Affiliate Marketing is cost effective.

Affiliate Marketing is the most cost effective when it comes to direct marketing option. Other direct marketing options like multimedia, billboards, and pay-per-click advertising maybe effective but are also expensive. There is no budget wasted when it comes to affiliate marketing since no payment is needed to be given to an affiliate unless a visitor they prefer becomes a customer.

2. Businesses using affiliate-marketing runs on a fixed costs only.

   There is no budget wasted when it comes to affiliate marketing. The amount paid to the affiliates is the cost of sale. The business owner will set the bounty and they will only pay when sales are made.

3. Brands, products or services are visible.

   High search engine listings can be secured by the affiliates and they can display advertisements in their websites. In referring customers, an affiliate only needs a website. This is a free brand, products or services exposure that does not have any down time.

4. Quick prospect and customer acquisition.

The affiliates can choose the ads they wish to put and advertise in their websites. These affiliates know who their audiences and future clients are. Because of this, they can pick the campaigns most suited to attract these prospects into their demographic. It is based on the affiliate's interests to pick the ads that the audience will mostly likely to respond to.

5. Marketing teams are outsourced.

Most affiliates are experts when it comes to search engine marketing, which will provide you a way of chance of getting to the top of search engines like Google or Yahoo without the need of spending too much money on Search Engine Optimization.

Affiliate marketing is one of the fastest ways for small companies to be exposed to the market since advertisements can be placed on various websites. Businesses can also save time in affiliate marketing since there is no need to search and find potential customers anymore.

6. Find-ability.

Once a consumer visits search engines like Google and Yahoo, multiple listings will be directed and link to the business, which will provide a better chance of being found compared to the other competitors who only have one to two links on the first page.

7. Return on Investment is transparent.

Businesses have the ability to track the origin of their sales. You can see exactly what, where, and when a sale is made.

8. Possibilities of earning in affiliate marketing are endless.

One of the fastest ways to start a home-based company is by affiliate marketing. In affiliate marketing, there are no limitations on the amount of income you can earn. There is no financial risk in signing up for affiliate programs too.

9. You Work At Your Own Time.

When you start affiliate marketing, you are also the one setting up your own working hours. When you work for a boss, you work when they tell you. There might also be times when they will ask you to work after your working hours just to have a job done.

Working at your own time means you can choose the ideal time when you think your body will be at the peak of its concentration. If your peak time is from 6 in the morning until 10 in the morning, then, you can work during those hours. You may just choose to resume your work again in the afternoon, during your peak hours again. If you are working for a boss with a dictated time frame, you cannot choose to work with your body, which may affect your work nonetheless.

10. You can measure your progress.

You can easily see the numbers of your audiences, the products you created and sold, and the profits you are making.

11. You can choose the products and the projects you want to work on.

You do not have to do the projects you are not interested in. You know those things you have passion on and the things that can make you successful. You do not have to force yourself doing something you do not really know or the things you do not want to work on.

12. You can do affiliate marketing anywhere in the world.

This is applicable for people who are working online. You may start building your empire in Greece. There will also be nod reason why you cannot write and finish the article you are making in United Kingdom.

13. Getting out of the job is not possible.

> There may be times when you will run out of clients or projects to work on. However, this instance will not make you feel unsecured and scared that you will receive a piece of paper and there will be someone to escort you outside the premises of the building.

14. The cash flow is endless.

> This is definitely one of the biggest advantages of affiliate marketing. Although working for someone else will guarantee you that you will get a pay check every 15th and 30th of the month, you would need to do your job competently, go to work early, and do all the things that your boss would like you to do. However, the amount you will receive is just limited to your salary only. When you work and market through affiliate marketing, the sky is the limit as long as you are successful on the things you are doing.

15. You are learning self-discipline.

> If you are already a personally discipline person, then, working for yourself is already an advantage for you. There may be some times when it is quite difficult to motivate

yourself to do what you would need to do. There may also be some times when you procrastinate and find some distractions which will keep you away from finishing a project you would need to submit within the day.

Working for yourself means you would need to divide your time for yourself as well as for your tasks and projects. It does not mean that you would need to allot more time for your job – it just means that you would need to have more discipline to finish your projects first to avoid rushing before the dead line while enjoying your own quality time.

16. You are the commander of the ship.

Have you ever experienced that you made a presentation then things turned sour and your boss started pointing fingers at you for the unsuccessful job? Of course you made the presentation but all the data on that presentation actually came from your boss. However, since you are just an employee, you do not have any other choice but to take the burden that should not be blamed onto you.

With affiliate marketing, you can choose to develop your niche. You do not need to follow what your boss wants simply because you are the commander of the ship itself.

17. You are earning extra but at the same time doing what you really love.

   A nine to six job might be quite boring for other people but there are also some times when you do not really have any choice but to stay with your traditional job. However, if you are using the Internet as a way not only to get out of your stress but also to unleash the hidden talent within yourself, you can also use it to earn a little extra. Remember, a little goes a long way! If you are using it to earn for yourself, then, who knows, maybe you can use it to earn and start using the job as a full time one!

18. If Affiliate Marketing Is Your Full Time Bread And Butter, You do not need to sacrifice your time for yourself. Your vacation time can be endless, depending on you!

   One of the downsides of working for another person is that you cannot take vacation as much as you want to. You would have to take some time and ask permission first if you can take a day off and just slug at the comforts of your home. There may also be some time when your boss will deny your vacation leave. How can you take away the stress that you are feeling? What if you will get more stress simply because you are just thinking about that vacation you would like to have?

Working through affiliate marketing means having more time for yourself. You may work for three weeks in a row but you can also take a time off and just relax and enjoy yourself. Take a vacation in the Pacific since you know you are worth it. You may also take a day off and just go to the nearest spa and enjoy all of their facilities. Your body will not only thank you – you will also feel more energized the next day too!

Andy Anderson

Chapter 4
Why Affiliate Marketing?

There are probably enough reasons to engage in affiliate marketing to write a separate book on the subject, but for now, we'll cover the most obvious stuff, then get you started on earning some cash and building passive or residual income – whichever you prefer to call it. Here, in no particular order, are the main reasons to go for affiliate marketing rather than other online earn5ing opportunities.

It's a portable, flexible, global thing

Like most online-based activities, affiliate marketing can be done just about anywhere in the world where there is an Internet connection. It is a new trend to work flexibly and have the opportunity to work from any place you like. Gone are the days when people would have to check into an office for their work and manage two to three separate jobs just to earn a minimum income for themselves or for their family. With affiliate marketing, it is possible to work from just about anywhere. And in these days of free WiFi, that means pretty much everywhere! So, you can sign up to a new affiliate, or keep an eye on your progress even when travelling if you want to. This is especially relevant to those that have a publicist's job. The travelling can be on the greater side and for them, it is possible to use their travel time and put it to productive use. You can indulge in marketing activities.

You're 'open all hours' once you get into affiliate marketing, and since you don't have a fixed place of business, you can take it with you wherever you go. So it's like you are a café that is open all 24 hours of the day and night and your business will not cease just because you closed your laptop. You will continue to make money regardless of whether you are active and sitting in front of your computer or lounging around, once you get yourself into affiliate marketing. Your working hours are flexible too – you can work while all around you sleep, and use you program as a second stream of income to supplement your salary. Or if you're a stay at home Mom, you can spend some time working when the kids are asleep or at school. So it is a portable and flexible line of business that you can use to help earn a few extra dollars on a monthly basis without having to leave the confines of your house.

And there is no hard and fast rule that says you cannot take it up if you are a professional. Affiliate marketing is for all. It is a great source of passive income and will at the least help you pay off your bills. It is a good idea to consider using the money that you make from this avenue to pay off a certain type of your bill, which will take off a little load from your shoulders.

If you're a retiree, or someone about to retire, looking for some additional income to supplement your pension, or a student aiming to fund a gap year or anything else in between, affiliate marketing could be just what you're looking for. All you have to do is sign up with a few companies and hold their ads on your blog, and you will have a chance to earn an income without having to put in any tremendous efforts.

Low start up costs and overheads

When it comes to starting a business, everybody starts to worry about the money that they will have to raise for it. They will wonder if they need to avail a bank loan in order to pump money into their business. Apart from the initial capital, there is also the worry of having to take care of overhead costs once the company is up and running. All these cause people to worry about having to start the business at all.

But the great thing about affiliate marketing is that, unlike regular business start-ups, you don't need a pot of money to get going. You do not have to worry about having enough money to start your business as you do not need to buy or rent premises, and that means there are no running costs such as rent, utilities, local government taxes and staff.

Now imagine somebody coming over to your house with a large banner and saying please place this on your door or gate and we will pay you money for it. Affiliate marketing is comparable to that scenario. You will not have to shell out money to start having your tie-ups and can do so without investing a single penny.

Now you may wonder how you will place something so big on your humble door and whether it will cost you to get it up and the answer is no! There is no need for you to worry about the money aspect at all. There is no company out there who will want you to shell out money for them to benefit from it. More importantly, there is nobody who will be willing to part with their money in order for another person or company to benefit from it. And so, you should care very little for the costs that you might incur if you decide to take up affiliate marketing and you do not have to worry about its upkeep and maintenance costs either.

It is like getting gifted a business and you are the sole proprietor except that, you do not have to pay for any of the company's operations.

You don't need to purchase or store large volumes of stock either – somebody else has that worry. All you have to do is sprinkle links on your website and wait for the clicks to come. Easy, isn't it? You get the salesman's commission, but you don't have to physically make the sale. You are the virtual salesman and don't have to run around from door to door to sell a product or service either. That way, you get to save on just so much time, energy and effort that you can invest all of it in doing something much more productive.

Little or no admin

When it comes to owning a business, there are a million small things that you have to consider in order for your business to thrive. One such small thing is "administration". Now what does administration mean you may wonder, well, let us find out.

Okay, you have no premises, no stock and no staff. Know what that means? That means you don't have to store and display the goods, or persuade the customer that what you're selling is exactly what she wants. And you don't have to worry about the customer returning goods for refund or replacement, because you're not actually selling anything. That's somebody else's problem, not yours.

These are the things that a storeowner needs to look into and not the job of a marketer.

Just like how you need not worry about the costs of hosting, up keeping, maintaining promoting etc. you don't have to worry about the administration of your business. Your company will take care of all of it and all you have to do is lure your viewers into clicking on the ads. Imagine how interesting it would be for you to simply write on your blog and another company pays for its up keep and smooth running. Will that not be an extremely thrilling prospect? You don't have to worry about the headache that regular business brings along.

If the business runs online – as many do these days – you don't need to process payments or packages and ship orders. And you don't need to chase up late payments either. So it is just the ideal way to run a business – not do anything yourself! I know it sounds almost impossible to pull off such a thing, as all you are being told is to host someone and get paid for everything related to it. But that is what sets affiliate marketing apart from the rest. This ease of operation for the Webmaster is what makes it such a lucrative business.

You have the liberty to choose your products and services.

When it comes to affiliate marketing, you do not have to do the projects you are not interested in. You know those things you have passion on and the things that can make you successful. You do not have to force yourself doing something you do not really know or the things you do not want to work on.

It complements your website.

Whatever your interest or niche is, you need content for your website, and affiliate marketing can help with inspiration and add an extra dimension to your site. For example, if you're a keen camper, and you sign up to an affiliate program with a well-known camping and leisure retailer, it opens up a whole new world of content for you. As well as writing articles about your personal experiences, recommendations for camping grounds and 'how to' pieces, you can review new products and offer advice. All this adds weight and value to your own site or blog because people can read about your experiences and product reviews and make an informed decision as to whether or not to purchase with just one or two clicks on a third party blog or website.

Remember that everybody likes to have recommendations and prefers to hear about something from others. Around 40% of the people will trust someone else's judgment as opposed to their own and prefer to buy something if someone else is recommending it. What this does is helps in understanding the right choices to make. So if you are to say you bought a new hair gel and it is not just making your hair shiny but also reducing dandruff then more and more people are going to opt for the brand. The same way, it is important for you to show faith in the products or services that you are promoting.

Some people like to take it personally because they genuinely like the product and wish to promote it out of their own will. This will further add to the experience that the reader or viewer will avail, as it is important for them to connect to what they read. Understand that they are interested in listening to what you are saying and then subscribe to the product by clicking on the link. So essentially, you are helping in getting the word out there and also getting a chance to have an opinion on it.

Just make sure you don't overdo the sales pitch – your readers want to learn from you above all else, so keep the mentions to a minimum. Think of it as a subtle way to drive across the message without being overtly intent on promoting something. Just plant the idea in the reader's mind and let it develop. And sprinkle the affiliate links sparingly – don't flood the site with them. The idea is to be as subtle about it as possible and not overdo anything.

Don't think it is your duty to over promote someone just because they are paying money for it. Think of it as a means to mutually help each other and that you are doing it because you have been asked to.

So, there are many good reasons for joining an affiliate marketing program, but a word of caution before you sign on the dotted line – don't just go for the first program that looks like it could work for you. It needs to be a good fit for your website, as well as providing you with a reasonable income. There can be some who will ask you to put in a hundred links and not pay you accordingly. You need to consider them carefully and either ask for more or ask for lesser links to be added. If you reach a consensus then well and good but if you have doubts about it then it is better to drop them and move to the next.

Remember that you need not think of these companies as being less in number and quite frankly, there is no dearth of companies that will be interested in hiring you for their affiliation. If you pass up on one then don't worry, as you will have the chance to affiliate with several others. As long as you are by yourself interested in the company's products and services, you will not find it difficult to promote them on your blog or website and also increase your personal reader base. After all, you are doing this for other people to read what you write and appreciate and if you are also getting a chance to make some money while at it, then it could not get any better for you.

Also, ask yourself if your website is a good fit for the program. Most of the companies don't really bother to go through what you are writing and will prefer to pick out blogs that are popular. So if some vague product or service website is approaching you then you can reconsider them. Taking the camping website as an example, you probably don't want to affiliate with a jewelry store, because the people who are reading your stuff on a regular basis are going to be looking for tents, sleeping bags and other camping essentials. Jewelry doesn't come under that heading. And your readers will not be impressed if they think you are trying to sell them something they don't need. So it is vital to have a direct connection with what you are writing. There can be some who think it will be a good tactic to put up vague ads just to deviate from the blog's topic. But this strategy will not work unless you have asked your friends to click on the ad. So the main point is for the two to connect at some level even if there is only a little connect. For example: tents and sleeping bags are the main things that people will be interested in no doubt, but you can also try slightly off beat things such as a solar burner or a solar milk shake machine, which will make it interesting for the readers. Remember, there are plenty of other camping websites to choose from, so don't drive them away with an ill-considered affiliate link. Make your choice carefully, and reap the benefits.

Andy Anderson

Chapter 5

Choosing an Affiliate Program That's a Good Fit

We've just mentioned how NOT to choose an affiliate program, but how do you go about choosing one that's a good fit for your website, that you are comfortable with, and that offers a good return in terms of remuneration? A lot of it comes down to old-fashioned common sense, but here are a few pointers to help you to make a good choice.

Remember that you need to find something that is a perfect fit for you and for this you need to consider certain things that will guide you and show you the right path.

Here are the various things you need to bear in mind for that to happen.

Avoid paid-for programs

When you type 'Affiliate Marketing Programs' into Google, you will be inundated with hits. Some of these will be companies who ask you to pay to join their program. They will make use of fancy pamphlets that you can download and mention a well thought for payment plan. What's more, they will probably offer you a huge 'discount' to climb on board. The program's normal sign up cost is $99, but for today only, you will be admitted for the special price of just $20 – it may even be less than that. They will in fact make it look extremely attractive by cancelling out the $99 with a big red cross and write $20 only next to it. So, what do you do? You close the window and move on, if you have any sense.

It goes without saying that there are a million suspicious websites out there all of whom promise you something but do something else. Now not saying that these people might cheat you, (actually, they will) but even if they are to charge you a high amount of money it will be for their profit and they will not be bothered about you or your website. So don't trust these and only trust your instincts into doing the right things.

As has already been noted, the affiliate business doesn't pay any commission to you until they make a sale, and remember this is a sale they wouldn't ace without your help. So why would they want you to pay for the privilege of widening their retail reach? It was mentioned before that nobody would be willing to part with their money just to promote someone else. It makes no sense for them to pay and buy the right to make money. That's like saying Microsoft wants to hire you but you need to pay them a fees for it.

I know it can sometimes feel like the right choice to make, especially if the website you visited is promising you many things. I am sure you have also considered it many times just to get started with affiliate marketing at the earliest. But who in their right senses would use their credit card details or check into their online banking account to transfer money to a spurious source? Not only is it dangerous for your account but what if you end up having an identity theft?

So as a rule of thumb, don't trust any website on affiliate marketing that promises you good business if you pay them some money first. That is not how it works and you will have to be approached in a different way in order for you to establish proper affiliate marketing set up. Remember, if you stay too long on a website you will tempted to check it out in detail. Instead, choose to exit as soon as possible and also clear your cookies.

Another thing that seems to happen is that companies who charge affiliates to join deal in high-ticket items. You may make a tasty profit from each conversion, but realistically are the people who will be visiting your site going to be interested in high-ticket stuff, even if it is linked to your niche? Even if you can answer 'yes' to that one, you're a beginner in the affiliate marketing game, isn't it better to make your mistakes for free? Because you're bound to make mistakes in the beginning.

Check out the business

We've established that any affiliate you pair with should complement and add value to your site for your visitors, as well as returning an income for you. We read on how it is possible for you to increase the number of customers that visit the affiliates page and how much more business both of you can establish together if you understand each other well.

But in order for this to happen, you must initiate the process of looking for the best affiliates to tie up with. So make sure that you do some research and try and choose the best one. After all, you have the choice to nod to or refuse a certain client depending on whether or not you like them.

One way to look for the good ones is by checking out what other blogs like you are hosting. You can randomly check the websites that other bloggers like you are hosting, especially the popular ones. Once you have a few, you can decide to contact them yourself and show them your blog or website. After you get a reply, you can skim through all the important ones.

Maybe you've looked at a few business websites and are wondering who to approach. You can decide to short list 5 or 6 of them and go to the next step.

The first thing to do is check out the website for navigation. Is it easy to find the products your visitors will be interesting, and how easy is it to complete the purchase once the affiliate link takes the reader to the product?

This is important because you have to believe in the website yourself before you decide to host them for others. You will have to place yourself in the shoes of others just so that you have a chance to look at your blog from a third party perspective. For this, you must understand how the affiliate website operates.

One way to check this out is to place an order on the site yourself, so you can check out the purchase process on behalf of your visitors. Is the navigation process straightforward, from adding the item to your virtual basket? Is it possible for you to edit the items present in your cart? Can you increase or decrease the volume of the products easily? Does it have an option to add in a coupon code? Is it possible to redeem any points? What about the payment process? Does the site support PayPal?

Many online purchasers are wary about using credit cards online, and prefer the speed, simplicity and security of paying via PayPal. And it's worth returning an item, so that you can check out their standards of customer service. By placing affiliate links on your site, you are effectively endorsing the company and its products to your followers, so you need to know they will get good service.

Imagine what would happen if you start putting links to websites that are slightly tough to navigate or the buying process is complicated? People won't be interested in clicking on the links and the company might not garner as many hits as is necessary.

Once you've checked out that side of the business, and are completely satisfied with what you have, it's time to speak to someone about becoming an affiliate, so that any queries you have can be addressed before you commit yourself.

Make sure you have everything sorted out and jot down the questions in terms of importance and priority. Once sorted, start asking them one by one if it is a telephone chat or you can also shoot them a mail with all your queries. Remember, it is never a bad idea to be well informed about something. After all, you are hosting their website and it is best that they give answers to everything that you wish to know. It might take them some time to get back to you and you can give them a couple of days' time to go through all your questions and answer them one by one.

If nobody is available for you, or they keep you waiting for several days for a reply, maybe you should move on. After all, if they can't make the effort to answer your queries before you become a partner, is it likely that they will do so once you've joined the program? So don't keep waiting on someone that is not keen on replying to you even if they say things like "sorry for the delay, we regret it".

What are the terms and conditions?

When you're happy that your chosen company will provide your loyal visitors with excellent service, it's time to talk about terms. After all, that's what it's all about. The first thing to ask is how the program works. Are you paid purely for sales, or do you get commission for leads? It is always better to argue for the latter as you will be tying up with someone who is considering you for your popularity. So it is best that you make full use of the opportunity and argue in your favor. It can make a big difference when it comes down to dollars, both in the amount you can expect to earn, and how long you will have to get paid.

How often do you get paid, and what is the minimum payout level? Many companies pay at the beginning or end of the month, or they may pay out twice a month – usually on the 15th and last day of the month. If you have a certain preference then you can consider asking them to change the time of pay out. Check that the minimum payment threshold is not set too high. Obviously, it's not cost effective to pay out every time somebody clears $10, but if you have to rack up $100 or more before you see the color of your commission, it can be very de-motivating, unless you have a high conversion rate.

Finally, you need to know the rate of commission – both the bottom line and the structure. Some businesses operate a two-tier system, where you get paid for everyone who clicks through to your affiliate, and then receive a further commission if they complete a purchase. Other businesses just pay for one or the other. Commission rates for affiliates vary considerably from less than one percent for clicks to as much as 75% for some digital download products. However, it's more realistic to work on a figure of between 5% and 20%, and it's worth comparing similar companies to see if their commission rates and terms and conditions are similar.

Remember that money is important no doubt but you will also have to consider several other factors that will help you judge whether the products and services offered comply with your standards. You cannot simply give anybody a nod and must lay down some ground rule for them. This might seem like a wrong thing to do but you need to maintain the standard of your blog and website as well. For this, you can send them a mail listing the things that you will not be okay with on your blog or site such as sexually explicit content, weapons, adult products etc. There can be companies who will be looking for people that will be interested in letting out some space for such items. If they suspect that you have not explicitly mentioned these terms then they might start supplying you with links to such products. So it is important for you to try and check everything that they send across just to be cautious.

You must also discuss the rights and obligations and agree upon a termination clause. Remember, if you follow a path that is extremely professional, then it will be easy for you. You cannot take anything too lightly or casually, especially during the initial stages. Make sure you have everything signed and attested just to maintain an official record of your alliance and agreement. Once you are satisfied with everything and have made up your mind to go ahead with the deal then there should be nothing in your way to stop you.

So, having chosen your affiliate business partner, how do you go about actually earning money as an affiliate? The next chapter will get you started on earning money online and building up a passive income stream as an affiliate marketer.

Chapter 6

Making Money from Affiliate Marketing

The first thing to remember here is that, despite what the hype says, you will not get rich quick from affiliate marketing, although it is possible to build up a regular stream of income if you tackle it right. So don't expect to become a millionaire overnight. You will have a chance to supplement your regular income.

That's not that the claims that you can make four figure sums are not true – just that it isn't going to happen overnight, so get used to that idea. Yes, you can make money while you sleep, without doing a thing about it, but it's likely to be cents not dollars, at least in the early days while you're learning your craft. And make no mistake; there is a skill to this. These are the things to keep in mind if you're serious about making money from affiliate marketing and following on these will make it easier for you to see your ambition through.

Build your website traffic first, and be patient

Before we look at how you can start making money out of your affiliates, let us look at what is required by the companies to hire you.

Affiliate marketing thrives on people's interest in clicking on links to products that catches their eye. But who are these "people"? Well, these are people who will visit your blog or website to read what you have written. So in order to lure these people, you have to make your blog or site as interesting as possible. It is fine to go all out and decorate it as much as you like. But make sure you keep with the theme otherwise people will only visit to mock your blog.

Remember that you need to establish a good reader base in order to land an affiliate marketing gig.

So, it's no good setting up a website today and joining an affiliate marketing program tomorrow. Until you're getting a good number of unique visitors – or impressions - to your website, you're not going to get the click-through to your affiliate. Here, "unique" refers to new customers and not the same old ones who have probably book marked you and keep visiting all the time. You must have had several of your friends telling you to check out your blog or site and also asked you to visit often and spread the word. Well, they are doing this so that their site or blog has enough "traffic".

Clearly, not everyone is going to click on the links, and to get a reasonable amount of clicks, you need plenty of regular visitors. You also need to build up a reputation as an expert in your niche before people will trust you enough to go for your recommendations. It is like running a site that throws up one interesting piece of writing after another in order to lure people into reading it and staying put. That is exactly how your website should operate. There should be interesting content for people to read and remain glued. It is not helpful if they visit just once and immediately forget about your blog.

You need to track the number of people that visit your page and record the numbers per day, per month and per year. This will help you in knowing how popular your blog really is.

So what happens when you have got enough visitors? Before you ask, nobody seems to be sure what constitutes 'enough' in this case. Some people say 1,000 impressions a month; others say 1,000 impressions a week. So it is safe to assume that having at least 4000 to 6000 impressions a month will help you in becoming popular enough. Well, then you have to be patient, because it will take time to build up revenue. Remember that it is always cumulative and for the number to go high, you need to wait it out. You're not going to be making $1,000 dollars while you sleep at the end of the first week. In fact, it could be months or even years before you get to that stage, if you ever do (but hey, nothing wrong in dreaming big, right?). And you certainly won't pull in the big bucks with just one website. Play the patience game, and take the time to learn what works and what doesn't before you dive in with both feet. The more prepared that you are, the better the results that will come your way. Putting in a little hard work at the very beginning will help you go a long way in establishing a good line of passive income. Don't worry; with all the hard work you put in, it will be worth the wait – honestly!

One good product or business is enough

Now that we understood who these "people" are that will help you in having a good traffic come your way, let us look at what they will be interested in.

Newcomers to the system often make the mistake of peppering their site or sites with lots of different things, imagining that people are likely to buy more because they have more choice. It is typical human thinking to want a lot of choice in anything and everything, let alone links on a website. But then, this is wrong on so many levels. You are not a store – you don't have to offer your customers choice, because they did not land on your site with purchase in mind. They're there for information, and if you're good at what you do, you'll be able to persuade them to buy something while they are there so you can make some cash.

Think of it as a classy gig to have only one website promotion and that website is the best one that your readers can have. That is, you will have the chance to promote one product or service better rather than having to do it for 5 or 6 different ones. Not only will that confuse your customers but will confuse you as well. You will have to look into two or three different companies and think of where their links will look the best. So in effect, you will be complicating the process for yourself. It is better to have faith in one product or service and promote it to the best of your abilities. Think of yourself as a pop up store to promote one product as opposed to a super market that offers a lot of choices.

Sticking with the camping website example, in this instance it would be a good idea to affiliate with a business that retails camping and leisure goods, rather than a single product. Say you write a review article on the latest in winter sleeping bags. You can point out the virtues and problems of a product sold by your affiliate, and if you pitch it right, they'll want to buy one. Because they can do it easily from your site, they'll click through, and maybe buy something else as well while they're at it. Result!

As was said earlier, it is always the power of suggestion that works on a majority of the customers. They will take a liking to something if you tell them that you are offering them the same product that you have personally tested and liked yourself.

On the other hand, it there's too much choice – say you've got links to half a dozen different sleeping bags, as well as the one you've reviewed – they'll go to a price comparison site to check things out. Once they leave your site, it's unlikely they'll return, so you've lost the sale – and the commission. So don't make the mistake of putting up too many choices at once. If you have put up just one and the website is offering it at the best price in the market then even if the person has left your site to do a quick price comparison, he or she is sure to return back to yours to click on the ad.

Also, focusing on a single product or business makes it easier to make keywords work for you. As was said before, you will get confused if you have too many products and services to promote. Make it simple for yourself and maintain just a few links.

So, stick with one business or product. If you want to do more, set up a different website for each affiliate, and concentrate on that, rather than spreading yourself too thinly. What you can then do is, try and link your sites. So that way, there is no bombarding the customer with too many things at once and you have the chance to put all your work on display. Remember, if they really liked what they bought from one of your site promotions, then they are sure to check out your other sites and click on the ads placed there to check if they like something from it. So just by reducing the choice that you put out for your customers/ readers, you will have a chance to maximize the benefit of your business.

Content is king!

This is true of any website of course, but it's especially relevant if you are hoping to make money from affiliate marketing. People go to websites to be informed or entertained – often both at the same time. So, make sure you have plenty of content structured around the products or business you are promoting.

Another point to remember is that search engines can tell whether there's quality content on your site, and will rank it higher as a result. That means more visitors, and hopefully more sales.

You must be well versed with the concept of "SEO". SEO refers to search engine optimization. You must have heard that many companies have a good SEO team that helps them in turning popular. Well, this is true because these teams will work hard in promoting the websites and blogs of the company and help it appear on top of the Google search list.

For this to happen, you need to pick out all the top words from your blog or website, that are most likely going to be typed by people. If they get the combination of words right then your site is going to appear as the top most links. For this, you can also make use of a small description that will help you put in all the main words.

But remember just a good SEO description will not do the trick and you need to have a good content as well.

By content, we mean stuff that's worth reading, and that will be informative for the reader. So forget about the keyword-stuffed sales pitches when you are coming up with the content for your blog – educate, inform, entertain, but whatever you do, don't spam. You don't need long articles – in fact, three hundred word posts will hold the attention of your audience better than one 800 – 900 word post. The more information you give away; the better the reader base. Most people will look for sites that will give them an in depth look at difficult topics. By making it easy for them, you will have a chance to increase your reader base.

You need to be as different and unique as possible so that people don't get what you offer elsewhere. For example, if you wish to provide customers with recipe ideas then come up with good and unique ones that are not easily available on the Internet. If you wish to give them cheesecake recipes then make sure the ones you offer are unique and try off beat flavors such as lemon chilly cheesecake. Once they take a liking to your unique recipes, they will be interested in clicking on an ad in your site, which might be a particular cream cheese brand or even baking trays. You can also explicitly mention that you have used these brands and hyperlink the products with the words. Your readers are sure to click on them!

There are some people who will start out well but their quality of work will start to go down. Your loyal readers might return no matter how bad it gets but you will have a tough time getting new ones to read. So try and maintain your site and don't allow it to go awry. Your quality is what made you popular in the first place.

Keep the posts on topic, and plant the idea in the reader's mind that they need to buy whatever you're promoting. You can even drop a contextual link to a particular product in the post —

research shows that people are more likely to click contextual links than separate buttons on the side bar. Help them to reach a decision, rather than trying to direct them straight to the sales site. The soft approach is the best approach here as you are trying to be subtle about your promoting. I am sure you yourself have bought many things by clicking on ads put up on blogs and sites that you read. So just think of those incidents and craft your affiliate marketing business around it.

Promote your site

This sounds obvious, but if you want people to come to your site, read your content and click on your affiliate links, you need to let them know the site exists. Whether it is a product or a service, everything needs to be promoted in order for people to be aware of what you are doing.

Without proper promotion, how are you going to get word about your website out there? There are only so many friends that will click on your links and in order for you to land a big gig; you will need at least 1000 clicks a week. So what is it that you can do to promote your site? Well, let us find out!

Firstly, list your site in search engines, write press releases to be distributed online, and promote your site on forums in your niche and social media.

If you have a friend whose blog is extremely popular then you can consider asking him or her to subtly promote yours on theirs. But you might have to consider paying them a small fee for it, as you will be benefitting from their service to you. If you don't have any such friends but know of someone who has such a blog then you can consider contacting them and asking them politely to promote yours. Again, promise to pay them a fee for helping in promoting your blog. Ideally, choose another blog that speaks on topics like yours or something on the same lines.

It's a good idea to have Facebook and Twitter accounts linked to your website, and set up so that each time you post an update on the site it's posted to your social media account. You can also have a Facebook page dedicated to your website or blog where you will keep updating with links to your site. It is also a good idea to like the pages of the products or service that you are promoting. This will again help people make a connection and chances of them clicking on the ad will increase. Make sure you update the page from time to time and not merely have it as a fancy advertising tool to own. Many people start out enthusiastically but fail to keep up, and you surely don't want that happening to you.

Work on building an army of followers, but don't even consider buying them. Bought followers are not going to go to your website and click on the affiliate links – they just give the false illusion that your social media account is more popular than it really is. You might think of being popular but once the bubble bursts, you might be extremely disappointed. It's an illusion and a fake, and if you're going to succeed in affiliate marketing, you have to be credible and trustworthy. If it is a group of friends then make sure the group is genuinely interested in your blog or site and are not doing a favor. Those will only last for a while and decide to abandon you once they lose interest. So try and find a diverse group who will not lose an interest in your writing and don't force anyone or buy anyone for the job.

You cannot cheat your readers or your marketing partners. Remember, you will reap what you sow and so, it is best that you remain as honest and trustworthy as possible.

Don't be invisible or anonymous

This is a golden rule. First and foremost, you have to have confidence in who you are and what you do. If you don't have self-confidence then it will not work in your favor. Imagine what would happen if you had to address an important crowd consisting of your potential clients and you don't have the confidence to reveal your true identity, will that not work to your disadvantage?

So, just because it's easy to hide behind an alias on the Internet, it doesn't mean you should. It can be tempting to use a cool name but don't do so. If you want to build credibility and earn money online, you have to be seen as a real person, with proper contact details. Don't hide behind a pen name or a nickname, use a real name and an email address tied to your domain name, rather than a Hotmail or an AOL account. If you wish to use a pen name then consider putting it in brackets so that the person is aware of your real name as well. Make sure you write out your full name including initials, as there can be many others with the same name as you.

Many people think it is unsafe to advertise their names on the Internet. There were also stories doing the rounds of how unsafe it really can get. But, there has been a lot of awareness and the problems it might cause are not really relevant or big enough.

Remember that people need to know they can contact you with questions, and that they will get an answer from a real person. They might also ask for a genuine photograph just to be sure of who the other person is. If they can't trust the Webmaster, they're not going to click on the affiliate link and you won't make any money. It's all about trustworthiness.

Remember how you were advised to reconsider a client who did not reply to your queries? Similarly, the client will have doubts in terms of who to trust and who not to and might definitely not trust someone that they think is hiding their true identity.

There is a theory that people are going to get hired more if they have completed their profiles and have also put up a recent photograph of themselves. This means that the person is trustworthy and the client will be happy to consider them for the job. So bear this important point in mind when you decide to take up affiliate marketing and fill out all the details in your profile.

Before you start to make money from affiliate marketing, you need to have your site set up to encourage people to click through on the advertising links. That means having great content that's informative and/ or entertaining, earning a reputation for being an expert in your niche and taking a soft approach to selling. Let your knowledge and enthusiasm persuade the reader to click through, rather than filling the site with banners and sales pitch. Also, be sure to provide proper contact details so your readers know you are a real person. Now you're ready to sell, but what are the best affiliate products to sell, and how can you get started?

Andy Anderson

Chapter 7
Myths about Affiliate Marketing

Your first thoughts when you think about digital marketing are SEO, Landing Page Optimization, PPC, and various other channels. But when we do this, we ignore of the most effective tools of digital marketing, which is affiliate marketing. Affiliate marketing has revolutionized the way businesses are being run these days. Before you brush off this as another marketing gimmick, it is essential that we bust a couple of myths about affiliate marketing. Let us take a look at these myths.

- **Affiliate marketing is extremely difficult**
Well, many people are of the opinion that affiliate marketing is extremely difficult. But all you need to do is spend some time and gather all the required information about this. And then you will be pleasantly surprised when you realize that,

you need some time, information and willpower to get started on this path. You might not be able to make a splash immediately, but you will eventually get there. So this myth about affiliate marketing is not true. You need some focus to set your foot in the right direction.

- **Affiliate marketing is quite simple**

Yes, I know this sounds contradictory especially after saying that affiliate marketing is not difficult. It is true that affiliate marketing is not difficult, but that does not mean that it is extremely easy either. You will need to put in some effort; you cannot expect to earn a profit or even an income if you set up a substandard website. Like everything else, you will need to put in some hard work if you want to enjoy the benefits later on.

- **You need to find a niche**

It is always advisable that you select a market that you are comfortable with and also have an affinity for it. But this does not mean that you restrict yourself to only the small space or niche you have created for yourself. Select a niche that works best for you, it can be small or large, or it can be one that would offer a group of related small niches. Select the best possible niche out of the available options.

- **The good niche markets are already taken**

Don't fret. No, not all the good niche markets are taken, so calm down; there is more than enough space for everyone. While searching for a niche you are zealous about, it is not uncommon that you might discover that particular niche is already saturated. So, what you can do now is select a related or an associated niche or even a secondary one. Well, if you are one of those individuals who don't mind facing competition, then you can go ahead and establish the business you are enthusiastic about.

- **Only one affiliate program**

If you have selected a micro niche, it might feel like you have got only one choice for selecting an affiliate program. But it is in your best interest that you select more than one affiliate program, provided that you can. The mentality of the customers is such that they would like to price shop, so make this option available for them.

- **You need all the affiliate programs available**

Yes, I know that I asked you not to restrict yourself to only a few affiliate programs, but that does not mean that you decide to take on all the available affiliate programs. Well, the number of affiliate programs you select depends upon what your aim is. If you were a sharp shooter or a sniper, then you would have specific targets. But if you think you would rather use a machinegun and see the number of targets you will hit? Then go ahead and select as many programs as you want to.

- **Affiliate marketing is not profitable**

Now, that is not at all true. In fact it seems silly. You need to plan out your strategies a little carefully, and then you can see the huge profits you can make. For instance, over $25 million was paid out as commissions in one year by a segment of ShareASale's merchants.

- **Easiest way to make millions**

Yes, it is true that there is a lot of money in affiliate marketing, and you will need a well-planned strategy to increase your net earnings. But this is not an easy task. It might even take you a few years to make this a source of full time income. And it is essential that you realize that, you might not make millions. But this does not mean that you don't stay positive. All it means is that you need to try harder and work harder to make your dreams come true. You never know, when you might hit a jackpot.

- **The market is already saturated**

Let us be realistic when we say the affiliate market has reached its saturation point. Well, can you think of any field in today's world that does not have any competition in it? The answer is a definite no. Similarly, even the affiliate market is a little crowded. But this does not mean that everyone is the market is doing well for themselves. A lot of individuals who set up their affiliate sites are not really doing a good job at it. Don't see all the flashy banners pasted everywhere. This doesn't mean anything. So be brave and take a plunge into the world of affiliates.

- **Affiliate marketing is nearing its end**

Hush! No, affiliate marketing will not come to an end. Yes, it will change, but it will not disappear. So the market is changing. There is nothing to fuss over. Change is a good thing, it will help you evolve your strategies and learn more.

These were some myths about affiliate marketing. And knowing that these statements are in fact not true would help you gain an ounce of confidence to take a step into the world of affiliate marketing. Affiliate marketing is here to stay and grow. And this is an excellent opportunity.

Chapter 8
Ways to Get Affiliate Links

One of the most common ways in which you can launch yourself into the world of affiliate marketing is by creating a website. And if you are in it for the long haul, then it would be in the best interest of your business that you create a website.

However, if you are still at the stage of learning about web designing or if you are amongst those who are not interested in creating a website, but still want to be a part of affiliate marketing, then fret not. There is an easy solution to this problem. And in this chapter you will learn about the various ways in which you can get started with affiliate marketing without the use of a website. Sounds incredulous, doesn't it? Just patiently read through this chapter and you will realize all the viable opportunities that you can make use of to get started.

Remember that the main objective of affiliate marketing is to provide you with a way in which you can put up your affiliate link in front of the target audience. Like mentioned earlier, building a website is the most common approach adopted. But then again, the path you opt for is entirely up to you. With this basic objective in mind, let us look at various methods that you can use for getting your affiliate link to the target audience.

Make use of blogs and forums

This is perhaps the easiest way in which you can test the waters in affiliate marketing. All you have to do is zero in on a product that interests you and you are keen on promoting, then start marketing this product by posting about it on various forums and blogs. The question is how do you direct the users to your affiliate link? Well, the answer is quite simple. Make use of your affiliate link as your signature. If you make yourself an active member on any forum and if you have followers then this will just be an added advantage. But then again, you should be cautious about the kind of blogs and forums you decide to post about your products on. You need to post on such blogs and forums that deal with a topic complimentary to your own product or at least along similar lines as what you are promoting. If you want to market about a fashion apparel affiliate product, then you might not find any enthusiastic supporters on a forum meant for car décor.

Along the same line of thought, if you are really interested in making a big splash on any public forum, and then you will need to be careful about the content you are posting. Ensure that the content is not only interesting but helpful too. Try becoming an active member on the forum. And once you have managed to establish yourself and garnered the attention of others, then more number of users would want to visit your link. And also maintain some etiquette while posting online. Don't spam the blog or forum with unnecessary posts, this might eventually lead to you being banned on the forum or even your posts might be deleted.

Try viral marketing

Have you heard of viral marketing? Yes, it a very popular way of spreading awareness about something very quickly. So, for doing this you will need to figure out a product that can go viral online. A viral product is a product that has been created with the ability to spread it quickly to a large number of people. This is one of the fastest ways in which you can gain attention for your product. What you can do perhaps is to write a very short eBook, preferably less than 30 pages or even a report on a particular topic that interests you, and then insert the links to your affiliate products in it. Then you can distribute it to the audience using your favored means. You could sell it, put it up on other websites or even just casually inform people that they can give it away. For starters, you can start selling this eBook on eBay for a nominal price. Ensure that whatever you are writing about is actually informational and useful. No one would want to go through a document filled with affiliate links. If your book is successful, then you have would have gathered a lot of attention for your product.

Make use of YouTube

Who hasn't heard of YouTube? YouTube is one of the most popular ways in which you can get your message across to literally millions of users within no time. YouTube has nearly a billion visitors every month. That is simply incredible. And you could very well use it to your advantage. All you need is a webcam, an innovative idea and Internet. These three things are more than enough to start your own channel on YouTube. You can insert your affiliate links in the description of your channel and even in your videos. In this manner, you will be able to convert your followers into affiliate users and this will generate profits for you.

Select a niche you are interested in, and once you have decided that then you can start a video series about it and you can insert your affiliate links in it. The viewers would already be interested in the video series created by you and in this manner it is likely that they would even be curious about the affiliate product you are promoting. There are two rules and you should abide by them if you want to use this vehicle successfully. The first rule is that the content you are posting should provide the viewers with some value and monetary gain for you should be a secondary objective. If you start the series with only the monetary aspect in your mind and want to make money from your link, then this behavior will get you listed, as spam and all the hard work you put into this will be useless. If what you have produced is meaningful and interesting, then the chances of gaining attention and even respect of likely users will increase. The second rule is that don't create something that is misleading. You would be violating YouTube's policies if the video you have posted is unrelated to the link or even if the title or description is misleading. This is something that you would want to avoid.

Video marketing on YouTube is easy, but then if you aren't careful then it can be quite risky. It is highly likely that the affiliate links can be branded as spam. So the best way to avoid this is by being honest and being useful. Ensure that you have quality controls in place and the content is meaningful; don't indulge in any behavior that can be listed as spam. If you are interested in nutrition then you could have instructional videos relating to cooking, you could even have discussions related to this topic.

Anything that might prove to be useful for the viewers is the best way to gain attention.

There are some precautions you can take to ensure that your videos aren't listed as spam. The first thing you can do is, try to not include too many affiliate links in your video. It is apt to include one link in your description and another one in the video, provided it is relevant. The second thing you can do is to mention that the link is an affiliate link or that you are an affiliate. You can also contact YouTube to ensure that you aren't in any trouble. If you have managed to acquire a valuable viewership then this means that the chances of making money from your affiliate links have increased.

Consider writing ads and reviews

You can use classified sites to promote you affiliate product. You must already be familiar with websites like craigslist, eBay and so on to look for any product you desire. The same can be used to promote you affiliate product too. You can write ads or even reviews about your affiliate products and then post them along with the affiliate link.

Consider building a Hub

One of the easiest ways in which you can get started as an affiliate is by building a Hub. And for this you needn't build a complete website right from scratch. A Hub is like a miniature of a website, it is just about a page. So in this page you can talk about anything that you are interested in, you can base your content on the affiliate market and related products you are interested in. your Hub would be put up on the HubPages site and it is perfectly alright even if you don't have any knowledge about web designing. You can still make it look decent and professional. The advantage of making use of Hub is that you don't have to code the page in HTML. You can create the page on any topic you are interested in; you can insert various ads, reviews or any other content that you want. Another good feature of this is that, it is even a social networking platform. Even being simply present on HubPages you can attract traffic towards the topic you are interested in.

Make use of pay per click (PPC) advertisements

This is not a method that would come as most recommended. In this method, you will have to create a lot of pay per click or PPC campaigns making use of search engines like Google, Yahoo, Bing, etc. and then you will have to promote the merchant website by making use of your affiliate link. So this is not a straightforward method. Instead of directly making use of PPC to promote your own affiliate link, you will send all this to your merchant.

There are two things that you will need to know about before selecting this option. It might just happen that the merchant website might not accept your affiliate link. You will have to compete with other advertisers for the space available. And you might as well forget about your ad if it isn't well written and it is not attractive and not just this but you will even have to bid an amount higher than the rest. And the second aspect is that you will have no quality control over the merchant's page. If the merchant website does not have proper content or it is off poor quality then you would probably end up paying a larger sum than necessary.

To summarize this chapter, there are a lot of different ways in which you can get your affiliate link to the target audience. And these are; making use of blogs and forums, viral marketing, YouTube series, making use of classified websites, creating a Hub and making use of PPC ads.

Chapter 9
Type of Campaign to be Used

By now we have established the importance need of affiliate marketing and the ways in which your business would be benefited if you use this. Now moving on to the next topic, you will need to select the type of campaign you would want to use for the various affiliate products. The main affiliate marketing types that you can make use of for fulfilling the objectives of the merchant are as follows:

- **Websites**

Not all affiliate websites are useful for the merchant; there are some that will provide you with an easy access to your target audience. These are the kind of sites that you would want to take up. For instance blogs about lifestyle are considered to be as the ones that attract high quality traffic. Merchants might even encounter different varieties of websites, within these affiliates and these send newsletters on a regular basis to the users who have registered with the site. These newsletters are a means by which the interaction between the users and the site can be increased and encouraged. This interaction helps in increasing the rate of conversion into sales and such affiliates are very useful. This was from the perspective of the merchant, as an affiliate marketer you will need to develop your website by keeping this perspective in mind.

- **<u>Cash back sites</u>**

Such sites usually have a database of all the users who are registered with them. In this scenario, the merchant would offer such a site a commission at an agreeable rate for providing space to feature their deal. And in turn, the cash back site would offer its users cash back incentive, in the form of a special offer. The cash back site would then assist in making the sale and later on divide the commission received from the merchant with the users who made the purchase. These cash back sites are of two basic types. The first type is such a site that would give you your money back directly and the second one is where they provide you with credits that you are eligible to spend on, on your later purchases of products or services offered.

- **Marketing via emails**

There are some networks of affiliates that have entire databases filled with information about all those users who are registered with them and all such users who are willing and comfortable with the idea of receiving emails and various other commercial messages. This is extremely useful for the merchants because they will be able to segregate the target audience by taking into consideration various criterions.

- **Co register**

In this case the users who are registered with an affiliate are complying with the idea of their information being shared with another merchant for purely commercial purposes. In return, these users can subscribe to special offers that are provided. This is a very useful means, because in this case the user is signing up for some benefit or a perk that the said individual is already interested in.

- **SEM**

SEM stands for search engine marketing. In this method the affiliates would offer a means of PPC (pay per click) advertising.

- **Hot leads**

This is a new concept. Hot leads are generated when a specific campaign is addressed to a particular individual or even a group of similar individuals who have shown interest voluntarily towards the acquisition of the product that was being offered and they are likely to make the purchase without much persuasion.

Various methods of payment and the way to measure them

Four types of methods of payments usually measure affiliate marketing and these are as follows:

- The first one is CPC or Cost per click and in this method the cost is established according to the number of visitors of the web page have clicked on the affiliate link to arrive at the page of the merchant.

- The second method is CPL or Cost per lead. In this method the cost is established by taking a total of all those visitors who have signed up for the newsletter or otherwise have shared with the site their personal information.

- The third method is Cost per sale or CPS. And like its name suggest the cost is arrived at depending upon the total number of sales that have been made because of activity on the affiliate link.

- The fourth method of payment is CPA. CPA stands for cost per action and the cost is determined according to the number of actions that have been completed by a visitor on the affiliate site.

Once you have selected the type of campaign that you will need, one that is best suited for your particular needs then the next step is to make sure that the landing page is fully optimized and thoroughly prepared to be able to handle the conversion of the internet traffic into full sales. And lastly but not the least, there is one other extremely important thing that you will need to do for your affiliates. As a merchant, you will have to welcome them. This can be done by sending in a simple email that contains all the information they will likely need and this will also help in clarifying any doubts they are going to have.

Andy Anderson

Chapter 10

Strategies in Earning Money from Affiliate Marketing

One of the greatest places to generate income without the need of having your own products and services is through affiliate marketing. In affiliate marketing, the only thing you have to do is to direct the visitors and potential customers through your blog and traffic these customers to someone else's website or blog. Basically, just just referring the customer to another person will reward you.

There are several ways where you can get money as an affiliate. You can try the following methods on how you can get money through affiliate marketing:

1. Creating a YouTube video or blog reviewing a product.

Blogs provide useful reviews, articles, and product reviews for different consumers. When a potential client search for a product or service he is interested in, he will find the reviews in your blog, purchase the product or service link to your blog and you will be paid a commission for the sale. However, the challenge in creating blog sites is the increasing difficulty to rank a website or blog in search engines such as Google and Yahoo. It requires long term commitment since it takes several months of effort in publishing high quality articles that will help people.

The easier way to rank in search engines is to create a YouTube account and post videos pertaining to product reviews and has an affiliate link to it in the description box, so if a visitor clicks it and purchase a product or service, then, the YouTube author will get commission from it. YouTube, which is owned by Google, has a higher authority than a new blog, making it easier to rank than a blog. Google always rank videos in their search engine, making YouTube a powerful tool to take into consideration and advantage of.

2. Promotion and review of products and services on your YouTube video or blog.

Another way in getting money through affiliate marketing is by promoting or reviewing products or services on YouTube or blog. Reviewing products or services are easier than to create new blog posts from scratch. Each blog posts created builds the authority of your blog in the search engine and drives more traffic into your blog. Sharing a product, event program or seminar can also be promoted in your blog or YouTube channel.

3. Promoting products and services to your email listing.

The final way to get money from affiliate marketing is through promotion of products and services to your email listing. Most blogs have a special listing where visitors can enter their e-mail addresses to get access to some parts of the site. Most blog authors add value to these signers by sending free content, samples, videos, e-books and even helping them to reach their goals.

When visitors visit your blog and read your blog articles, a lot of them will end up clicking the affiliate links of products or services you recommend in your blog, which will earn you some money.

If there is a product or service that you want to share with your followers, sending out an email to them regarding the recommendation is the best option. However, in promoting products to your email listing, keep in mind these two important rules to follow:

- ***Never recommend or promote a product you have not used personally or feel comfortable using.*** Instead of thinking about the money, put your followers first. If you recommend or promote a product that is bad, a lot of your followers will lose trust on you and will never believe in anything you will be saying again. Developing a lasting relationship with your followers is the key to success of affiliate marketing. Your followers will trust you if you are genuinely trying to help and drive them to success.

- ***Maintain equality between promoting and value.*** Your followers will get annoyed if you kept on sending emails for products and services promotions only. They will begin checking your emails less frequently and the possibility of them unsubscribing into your email listing is high. Focusing on adding value to your subscribers is the first thing to do. Promoting, on the other hand, can be done once in a while as long as the product or service will greatly help them.

Andy Anderson

Chapter 11

Disadvantages of Affiliate Marketing

Till now, we have looked at how profitable affiliate marketing is and what are all its advantages. But it is equally important for an individual wanting to take up affiliate marketing to know its disadvantages too. The disadvantages that might cause quite some trouble for a merchant are as follows:

- It is not unfair to call affiliates as good weather friends. When you happen to be a new discovery in the affiliate market, there would not just be curiosity but even delight about what you are offering. But after this initial phase the curiosity would wear off. Once the next business pops in it becomes increasingly difficult for the older ones to retain their business. And more often than not, affiliates tend to monitor their earnings quite closely. Not just once or twice a day, but multiple times a day. The serious problem this poses is that, the affiliates will start to get nervous when their earnings do not improve. And it quite difficult for the earnings to increase on a daily basis for a short duration of time. It is okay for sales to decrease, but then once it does, a fair number of affiliates would leave the market or move towards better networks and this would affect your growth.

- The share of commissions of affiliates and networks might just take away all your profits. You might be able to increase your sales by making use of affiliates but then you should also remember that they would wipe out your profits if you weren't careful. The commission for affiliates is usually around 5-10% and added on to this you will also have to pay the commission for your affiliate networks if you want to join them.

- As an ecommerce merchant, it might just so happen that your usual profits might suffer, because your sales are being redirected by affiliates. And this might be quite scary. As a merchant, you might have had significant amount of sales, even without making use of the affiliates. When you first make use of a certain number of affiliates, it looks like they are bringing in you a lot of sales. But when you look at the sum total of all your sales, it just looks like it really hasn't made any difference. So what could have gone wrong? It might just be that the affiliate has been able to manage and get the customers to visit your site after clicking a link with the affiliate code. This should have resulted in a direct sale for you, which is the simple understanding at least. The reason why this happened is because of the usage of a wide range of methods like SEO, SEM and also the creation of fake coupon codes, the affiliates have managed to get the customer to visit your website but only by clicking on the link of the affiliate alone.

- Affiliates might not even treat your brand with the same respect that you know it deserves. You might have spent a lot of your time and resources to develop a website that meets your requirements. Some of the common troubles that a merchant would have to endure because of affiliates would be misrepresentation of your offer and they might also distort your brand imagery. These are minor troubles but would give anyone a bad headache. It is usually the short-term course adopted by these affiliates that causes all this trouble.

Keeping all the troubles aside, affiliate marketing is a great tool. It needn't be discarded as being useless. Yes, there are certain pitfalls and therefore it is essential that you are cautious while making use of this tool.

Chapter 12

How to Select an Affiliate Marketing Website

In this chapter you will learn about how you can select an affiliate website by helping you understand the characteristics you should look for and what you can expect from them. The first question that one will need to have an answer for before getting started with affiliate marketing is why one should even study about affiliate marketing. It is quite important that you should be able to select a company that will provide you with the best available option for the services of affiliate marketing. And it is very important to understand these services thoroughly before you engage them. Affiliate marketing, like you are fully aware by now is a rapidly growing industry and with the increase in the number of online users, the scope of affiliate marketing also increases.

It is essential to understand the services provided by an affiliate marketing company so that you will be able to make an informed decision. A good affiliating company should not have any fee for signing up and they should also provide you with the codes for tracking your sales so that you can earn the deserving amount. The other services that should be provided by an affiliate marketing company are as follows:

- The first service should be the array of features that can be provided by the affiliates and it is important for all the parties concerned. Features are the much-required key components that help in creating links for the advertisements; they also provide tracking facilities and help the advertisers in selecting the right advertisements for the concerned traffic. There are a lot of service providers and companies that are sincerely working on improving the services offered and also the features provided to make them easier for access and also functional so that they can be made use of for increasing not just the sales but commissions too.

- Reporting features are those options that have been created by the affiliate marketing services to help you track the effectiveness of the advertisements. This helps the user in understanding what is working and what isn't; what is holding back your sales too. These options not only allow you to understand the source of the traffic directed towards you and the money that has been generated but also source where it originated. Before you select a specific provider, you need to take a look at the time frame and the format too.

- The companies and services engaged in this line of business need to provide their users with technology that is easy to use and navigate. Internet users have been conditioned to expect certain tools they would require to be always at their disposal at any given point of time. The services provided should be easy to use and understand. And once this happens, the affiliates will be coming back for more.

- The process of searching for the products you intent to promote should not only be easy, but it should also be quick. Many of the companies in this field have a variety of search options so that their user can search in different ways. It is essential that the search can be filtered so that the users can obtain the required products. So it is essential to have filters to facilitate in the search in a short duration of time.

- If you are a service provider, then your duty is not complete unless you offer customer support services and help facilities. All of the best companies will provide its customers with not just tutorials to get them started but also the support services to help and guide them whenever they come across any hurdles. And when they also take feedback from customers, the company can improve upon the services provided to earn customer satisfaction. It is quintessential to maintain customer satisfaction, if not the whole concept of provision of services is redundant.

There are various websites that are available online and these websites will provide you all the data essential for a user before they opt for a particular affiliate marketing website. And you should compare all the services offered before you select one.

Chapter 13

Finding the Best Affiliate Product or Service for You

By now, we have read on the things you need to consider when you wish to start affiliate marketing. Now, let us shift focus to the types of affiliate options that are available in the market and the ones that will suit your blog or site the best. Let us look at these in detail.

The best affiliate product or service for you depends on your interests, your niche and your personality. When making your choice, bear in mind that if you have an interest in what you're marketing, you'll enjoy promoting it so much more. It's no good affiliating to a poker website, for example, if you have no interest in gaming, just because the commission is good. When there are problems – and there are bound to be – you'll be more motivated to work through them if you have a genuine interest in the product or service. In that, you can consider promoting two or more products but remember to limit it to not any more than 3 or 4 at a time. Once you identify the best from the lot, you can stick to that one alone and terminate contract with others. These are some of the most popular affiliate programs.

Health and beauty affiliates

Health and beauty is a good niche to affiliate in, because although most of the products are not high ticket, you have the benefit of returning purchasers, so it's possible to build up a decent passive income in this niche.

It is no secret that the beauty industry has seen a considerable boom in the last few years. This is mainly because everybody has become beauty conscious and is constantly trying to improve their looks. It is obvious that they will need cosmetics for their up keep and for this; they will need information on the products.

So, if your blog is about weight loss, healthy eating, fitness or skin care, check out affiliates such as the Market Health Network, which pays a 50% commission on all sales, including recurring sales. Market Health sells natural health and beauty products including skin care products, vitamin supplements, oral hygiene products, and many more, through its various affiliate programs.

This will allow you to write on diverse topics and cut down on the monotony. Imagine what would happen if you have to write on the same topic all the time, it will end you reducing your creativity. But if you spread out your content and write on a diverse range of topics then you will have the chance to showcase your writing talent and impress a large audience. It is also a good idea to check out their products first yourself so that your readers will gain confidence. You can choose a particular product and test it out for your audience. You can click pictures of the product and also the review for it. This will help you connect to your audience better and it will make it easier for you to promote your affiliate links.

Also, Market Health's cookies last for 30 days, so if one of your click-through doesn't complete the purchase but returns to order within 30 days, you'll still snag the commission. Amazon's cookies only last for 24 hours, so you may lose the sale if they don't order right away. Other companies worth investigating are Bath-and-Body.com, which stores cookies for 90 days – one of the longest periods - MedStore online pharmacy and free Weight Loss.com, which offers 50% commission on sales. Remember, if you have heard about the brand then chances are a majority of your readers will also have heard of it. When it comes to beauty products, people generally wish to settle for brands that they have heard about, as it is safer to choose products that they know are reputed. So if you affiliate with some of the best brands then you are in it for the win.

However, if the brand is not really well known but there are a few who vouch for their effectiveness in skin or hair care then you can take the responsibility of making them look good and promote them to your readers. In fact, take it up as a challenge to promote a brand that is not really well known, as it will help you explore your writing and promoting prowess.

You can also have a fashion blog and make it your parallel blog. A lot of the clothing companies and also online clothing stores offer good commission to their affiliates. All you have to do is write on fashion and throw in a couple of pics to help you connect visually. You can promote products of brands that you personally use. As soon as you buy a product, review it and put links. With time, your merchant will be happy with the business that you are creating and might promote you to super affiliate status.

But make sure that the new brand is not your only affiliate as that might retard your growth. Mix it up and have one big brand like

The Body Shop and one new company and write about both in the same breath. This will help people relate the two and will consider clicking on the other affiliates ads as well.

Forex (foreign exchange) affiliates

When people think of starting blogs, there are a few standard paths that they take up. One such path is that of writing about travelling and blogging about new destinations to explore. For this, foreign exchange can be a lucrative choice.

Foreign exchange is big business these days. Everybody is now going global and it is possible to reach out to a wide audience by working on this topic. If you run a travel blog, maybe this is the right affiliate partner for you, and the commissions can be very lucrative.

Some forex affiliates trade as a club, and you may have to pay a membership fee, but with commissions ranging from $150 to $600+ per conversion, many people are happy to take that step mainly because of the high rate of returns that it offers. Remember, if there is a guarantee on something then it is worth considering. It was mentioned before to steer clear of anyone who asks you for money for the service they provide but if the money you put in is for membership then it can be considered. The only reason that they ask for it is for the upkeep of their club, and so that, you can continue with endorsing them

Forex Club pays a minimum of $200 per conversion and up to $300, and their cookies never expire. Forex Mentor pays 30% commission on every sale and cookies last for 60 days. So it is best to consider this option if you are in it for the long run.

But there is a problem here, many people wonder if they will be able to weave in forex into their travel blogs and wonder if they can promote it effectively. However, there is no need to worry about forex, as you don't have to be a person of finance to understand it. It is easy for you to write about it and all you have to do is sprinkle the links all over your blog.

And if you really happen to be a person of finance then it will prove to be extremely easy for you. There is a chance for you to provide people with information on the basics of foreign exchange and can also be available to solve their problems and answer their queries. Your blog can turn popular in no time, as there is a demand for people who can provide expert views and analysis. Your forex link ups can prosper if you put in the effort to speak about the technicalities of a certain subject and give people a chance to understand the intricacies of the trade.

You can also promote parallel forex trades such as traveler's checks and give an in depth view of what these are. The final goal is to educate the masses on the subject and make sure that they fully understand and click on the ad to derive a purpose out of it.

Food industry affiliates

The food industry is now booming. Right from ready to eat snacks to exotic ingredients, there are a lot of choices in terms affiliate marketing.

People are ready to buy anything that they think will give them a unique culinary experience. Add to it information being provided on what is best to be consumed and how it can be used.

So if you are a food blogger then it is best to tie up with food related companies. There is a wide choice available and you can choose a company that works best with the kind of food that you promote.

Pinch of yum is a good company to consider as they pay 50% commission to their affiliates. It will come as no surprise that the company now thrives thanks to the affiliations that it has with bloggers and website owners.

As long as you have good numbers for your blog, big companies will come rolling in through the door. You can approach big companies such as nestle if you are using a majority of their products in your recipes.

The same extends to Pillsbury, who might affiliate with your blog if it has to do with baking. As long as your affiliates make sense and you do a good job at promoting them on your blog, you are sure to experience elevated sales and inflated commissions.

You need not always blog about recipes alone and can also do restaurant reviews and other such things that are food related. You can also affiliate with restaurant chains that will pay you a commission depending on how many people visit them or order from them.

There is no limit to what you can do when you tie up with a food corporation. You can easily earn staggering amounts of commission, as food is a basic human necessity and something that will live forever. So once you have a tie up with a bigwig company, you can start reeling in profits. But, you will have to work hard at amassing traffic and the more the people that visit your website, the better your chances of running into huge profits.

If you are finding it tough to find a good affiliate partner then you can check out E-junkie. It is a website that hosts several affiliate marketing companies which will be interested in tying up with good bloggers. They will also not charge you or take a part of your commission. So it will be a good idea for you to tie up with them and reap the benefits of your affiliation.

Online dating affiliates

I'm sure many of you will not consider this and move to the next option. This is mainly because of the stigma associated with promoting a site that caters to dating or making two strangers meet. But hey, everybody needs a partner and if you are helping them in finding theirs then there is nothing wrong with it.

Internet dating is big business, and if you host a relationship or self-help blog, this could be a suitable affiliate partner for you. There is a lot of demand for blogs that give away relationship advice and those that help individuals connect to others in a proper way. It might seem like a rudimentary emotion to fall in love but some people have a tough time with it. Such people are sure to turn to blogs to seek answers.

If you convince them enough into listening to you and buying products or services that will help them in the process then you are sure to make your online dating affiliates work in your favor.

E-Harmony is one of the biggest players in the dating game, and it pays up to $188 for every signup. Other dating affiliates to look at are Pull Your Ex Back, which pays up to $128 per conversion, and Kasidie, a swingers affiliate that pays 35% commission for each month your referees remain members. This would be a good fit for an erotic fiction website, or a blog about sexual experiences.

There is no need to worry about your blog being pulled down. As long as you have the permission and advisories in place nobody can touch your blog. So don't allow any kind of fear to affect you and continue with educating the world. It is possible for you to be as creative as is required and remember, when it comes to fiction, you can go all out and make it as interesting as possible.

You need to, however, know the best places to add in the links, as it will be detrimental to your business. Placing the links at the wrong spots or not making it clear might cost you. So understand the business first and then weave it into your blog.

Again, you have the choice to control what is promoted and what is not. If you really want to keep it clean and cater to a wide audience that includes early teens then consider steering clear of adult content. Your writing style should be such that it helps youngsters connect to it and makes them want to buy something or sign up somewhere. In fact, it might be tough for you to get your readers to sign up and they might just click on the link to check the site out. For this, you have to lure them into signing up by saying things like, "it's free", "you will love the experience once you sign up" etc. All these will make them want to sign up just to have a firsthand experience of what is being promised to them.

Psychic and astrology affiliates

Till now, we looked at things that are quite common and something that most people wish to have but now, we look at something that is slightly off beat.

It was mentioned before that you need to be as unique as possible in order to attract a large audience. It is possible for you to have a large base that is only there because you are offering them something unique, which they might not find anywhere else. For this, choosing a topic like astrology can work to your advantage.

You'd be amazed how many people go in for this, so it's a good niche to get into. If you host a New Age or pagan blog, this kind of affiliate would make a good partner, and they pay pretty well too. Psychic Source offers psychic readings and pays a flat commission of $100 per sale. Kasamba is a long established company providing tarot readings, astrological forecasts and psychic readings. They pay up to $150 per referral.

All you have to do is write on the topic in detail in order for people to understand what it is that you are talking about. They should have a good idea about what they are getting themselves into. But just the fact that they have chosen to check your blog out is enough to prove their interest in it. So try and make the most of it and guide them towards psychic reading.

If you decide to go with this type of affiliate, it's very important to check out the credibility of the individual or company – even more so than normal, due to the nature of the service. Look at online reviews, and if there are a lot of negative ones, try another company.

It is also a good idea to take up Wicca magic as a topic. There is a lot of interest in magic and witchcraft and more and more people are turning to it to help them. You will have a good time writing about it and can also tie up with companies such as Underground witch craft secrets will pay you $58 for every sale that you make. All you have to do is sign up with them and start speaking about witchcraft and magic spells.

There are several other such sites that you can choose for your site or blog. You will have to do a quick Internet search to find the best ones. Again, please be sure to check the veracity of the website before you start promoting it. Even if one reader has a bad experience then they will stop checking your blog out and it is known how one lost customer is equal to 10 new ones. So try and maintain your reader base and give them the best possible experience online.

Remember that you audience is interested in actually taking up witchcraft themselves and so, you must speak to them in a way that will promote the craft. You can also post pictures of your own witchcraft rituals in order to give them a glimpse of what it takes to use the science.

Online gaming affiliates

Gaming has taken center stage and is something that is enjoyed by one and all. It is always a good idea to consider affiliating with gaming portals as they attract a lot of clicks.

Most online gaming is big business, whether it's poker, casino games or bingo. And the commissions for affiliates are particularly generous. If you host a gaming blog, you may want to link with one of these. Ignite Bingo offers a generous 66% revenue share to affiliates for the first 6 months, then there's a tiered commission system with the best affiliates taking 50%.

Poker Strategy is an online poker school paying up to $500 per referral, with a two-tier commission system. Best Pay Partners is a virtual casino affiliate paying 50% of revenue share, plus 5% for referrals on a two-tier system.

These are just some of the most popular and generous affiliate marketing programs around, but there are many, many more, covering a wide range of specialist niches. Whatever your area of interest, there is sure to be an affiliate marketing network that is a good fit for you, so take some time to do your research and check out all the options available to you.

You can decide to dedicate different blogs to different games. You can concentrate on one genre each and reach out to a bigger audience. As long as you have enough people reading, you will be in a good position to get at least half of them click on the ads. Make sure you make use of simple language so that they understand what you are talking about. But if you are addressing an experienced gaming crowd then make use of gaming terminologies to help them connect with you better.

You can choose something that interests you so that you can talk about it easily. Tie up with a game that you are well versed with so that it is easy for you to tell others about it.

Signing up to most affiliate programs is relatively simple, although you may have to wait until the company checks out your website to be approved. Some of these companies are multi-national outfits with huge turnovers and a reputation to safeguard, so they're going to check you out before they let you in.

That's good, because it shows the company cares about its reputation, and doesn't just take on all comers. That makes for good business practice, and it shows that the company is in the business of providing good customer service, as well as being concerned about partnering with the right kind of associates.

Make sure that everything is in place before you begin to promote the products or services you are offering. You should have a unique tracking ID that registers every click through from your site, so that you get your commission on all sales and sign ups. And check out payment dates, commission rates and tiers, minimum payment amounts and the length of time cookies are stored on the prospect's computer. Affiliate marketing, done properly, can be hard work and time consuming, so you don't want to miss out on commissions because of sloppy admin. Once everything is in place – get on and just do it!

Andy Anderson

Chapter 14
Affiliate Marketing FAQs

Let us now look at some of the common questions that get asked on the subject in order to understand the topic better. Remember that these are just some of the questions and it is not an exhaustive list.

What is affiliate marketing?

Affiliate marketing can be defined as a means of earning money by promoting another company's products and services. It is "affiliating" with the companies to avail an income. It can be considered a passive income, as you are not directly getting involved in the earning process. All you have to do is tie up with some of the companies and they will pay you money depending on how much business you help them in availing. Every time they have a sale thanks to you, they will cut you in on the profit that the company makes.

Is it a good place to start business?

Yes. Although it lacks the elements of a traditional business, it is possible for you to set up one by using affiliate marketing as your base. You will have a chance to set up an online business that will help you have a steady stream of income. It won't have a physical existence but your online empire will be just as profitable as any other form of business. In fact, many people think of this as a better option as they will not have to invest money to start an affiliate marketing business.

Who is it for?

Affiliate marketing is for anyone and everyone. As long as you have an online presence, and a strong one at that, you can get into the business. It is best suited for youngsters who have a popular blog and have several people reading it. It is also for housewives who have popular websites or blogs that are read by a lot of people. There is no age limit and students can also take it up. If someone is looking to have a passive income to secure their future and retirement, then affiliate marketing is a good choice. It is also ideal for people who have already retired.

How to get started?

It is easy to get started with affiliate marketing. You have to first start with a blog or website and fill it with things that people will read. Once you have enough people reading, you can start affiliating. For this, you will have to look for companies that will affiliate with you. Depending on your blog topic, you will have to look for the best companies to tie up with. These can be well known companies and you can visit their website to know how they affiliate with bloggers and what are the terms and conditions that they have.

Are there any websites to sign up for free?

Yes. There are many websites where you can fill up a form and submit. These websites will have a tie up with several companies that indulge in affiliate marketing. The form will ask you your basic details and it will not take much of your time to fill it up. The website might have some terms and conditions themselves and might want a part of the profit that you might make through the affiliate tie-ups. You will have to look into it in detail before you decide to sign on the dotted line.

What happens after form is submitted?

Once your form is submitted you have to wait for it to be circulated between the different companies. Once it is read by a majority, the website will mail you a list of companies that are interested in tying up with you. Remember that most of the websites do a manual perusal of the forms and it will take up to 3 days or more for them to get back to you. You need to be patient and not bombard them with queries. If you have any doubts then it is best that you clear it out before you fill in the submission form. Once your form has been scanned, you will be sent a mail.

Does it pay well?

Yes. Affiliate marketing can help you earn a substantial amount on a monthly basis. It is possible for you to supplement your regular income and have enough to save at the end of the month. But how much you make will depend on the company that you are tying up with. You might make $100 or $1000 depending on how popular your site or blog is and how well off the company you are tying up with is doing. You can have 2 or more tie-ups if you wish to make a substantial amount out of it.

When will I be paid?

Most companies pay on the 15th. When it comes to affiliate marketing, you might not get the same amount every month. It will differ from month to month, as the same number of people might not click on the ads. The amount you receive will fluctuate but you must try and achieve a standard number of hits every month. Anything above the standard is your bonus. The companies calculate how much needs to be paid out on the 5th of each month. You might not have a choice to get paid any earlier but it might be possible for you to request a later date for payments.

Is there a commitment?

No. Generally there is no commitment and you are free to stop promoting any time that you like. There is no point in continuing to promote something that you no longer wish to. If you think a particular affiliation is not working in your favor then you can consider ceasing its promotions. In fact, if you wish to cease promoting all the programs then you can do so. There are no legal formalities involved in terminating your tie up with a particular company.

Is there taxing?

That will depend on how much you are making in a month. You might have to consult your accountant to understand if you will be taxed. Your affiliate companies will not have any knowledge on it and neither will the websites that you wish to sign up with. You must consider a priority to check for taxes in order to be on the safer side of things. Generally, there is a tax levied if you earn a certain amount of dollar a month and you cannot escape the law as they can conduct regular checks to see if everybody is paying their taxes correctly.

These form the various FAQs that get asked on the topic of affiliate marketing and hope you have had yours successfully answered.

Chapter 15
Affiliate Marketing Precautions/ Things to Consider

It is no secret that you need to observe precaution with everything that you do. You need to be careful and consider a few things before you decide to start affiliate marketing. Here are the things to bear in mind before taking up affiliate marketing.

Research

Remember to always do a thorough research of all the companies that are interested in affiliate marketing. There can be hundreds of them and you need to do your research on which the best ones are. Even if it takes you forever, you will have to lay down the groundwork to establishing a permanent relationship with a good company. Do not blindly go with the first company that offers you an affiliation. Even if it looks like a good company, wait for other offers to try and weight out the pros and cons of each company. Rushing into something will only adversely affect you.

Traffic

When it comes to building a good traffic, you have to set yourself a very high threshold. Don't remain in the hundreds, as it will not be good enough. There are several good websites out there that are not able to indulge in affiliate marketing owing to not having enough traffic. This can happen if you are not promoting yourself well enough. As was mentioned earlier, you have to go all out to promote yourself in order to be seen by people. Once that happens, you will have a large reader base and companies will queue up to sign you on.

Brand value

Remember to always consider the brand value first. You must go through the details of the company to know whether they are well reputed. You can conduct a small survey amongst your friends and family members to check if they have heard of the company or used their products and whether they will use them if given a chance. That will give you a good idea and make it easier for you to decide. Also make sure you check out the website personally in order to know whether your readers will find it easy to navigate on the site and buy products, as they have to do so, in order for you to earn a commission for it.

Information

Remember to never give away any more information than what is required of you to provide. Some companies or websites might ask you things that are in no way related the contract and force you to divulge the details. But you need to be careful and not give away excess information on any topic. If they are being unreasonable then it is best to immediately stop and cut all ties with them. Don't think just by stopping affiliating with them will cost you, if you are good at what you do then you will have no problem in finding another company to tie up with.

Payment

Make sure you talk out everything that there is to in terms of the payment that you will receive for your services. Some companies will take you for granted and might not pay you enough or on time. You will have to be vigilant and make sure that your account is credited every month. Many people make the mistake of not checking if they are getting the money regularly. There might be some companies who will purposely not pay and wait until they are summoned. If they find out that you are not checking then they will surely take you for a ride. So make sure you keep track of the money that comes into your account and how many people are reading your blog and how many are clicking on the ads. This will especially be relevant if you are getting paid for leads.

Follow up

Remember to always follow up on all your contracts and agreements. You have to have a good rapport with the companies and be in constant touch with them. Don't shy away from calling them up or shooting them a mail if you have any doubts or queries. After all, they are tying up with you because they realize your worth. Make sure you follow up on the payments and maintain a record of how much money you make on a monthly basis.

Overdoing it

When it comes to affiliate marketing, don't overdo anything unless it is working to your advantage. This can include buttering up the company to pay you more or tying up with 10 to 12 companies. If doing so is working adversely for you then it is time to stop and take stock of the situation. But if it is only helping you make more money, then you can continue with it. But as a rule, start out with just 1 company and then move to another and so on. Keep going until 6 and then check if it is working in your favor. If it is not, then cut down on a few. There is no rule for you to continue on even if it is not working for you, and as was read earlier, you can terminate your tie up any time that you like.

Not doing enough

Some people start out enthusiastically and raking in huge profits. But then their interest starts to deteriorate and they begin to take their success for granted. Remember that you cannot establish yourself in the business if you do not keep up with your enthusiasm. Make sure that you remain interested in taking forward you business and do not stop doing a good job. Your popularity might start to deteriorate and it might get difficult for you to make your affiliate partners stay back. So don't take your success for granted and continue doing the good job that you are doing.

Diversify

It is a golden rule to diversify but make sure you don't have too much on your plate. You have to diversify in limit. Once you do, you will have a chance to appeal to a bigger audience base and this means more business. Try and go into different streams and not just stick to one type of subject. You will have the chance to tie up with two or more big companies who will be catering to different topics.

Critics

Remember that there will always be others who will critic you but you must remain confident in everything that you do. Simply giving into critics and their opinions will be useless. They are obviously doing it to throw you off focus and affect your work. Remain as strong as possible and not give into anything that people opposing your success have to say.

These form the precaution/ virtues to bear in mind when you decide to take up affiliate marketing and have a good time making money through your affiliations for a long time.

Chapter 16
Affiliate Marketing Jargons

Although affiliate marketing is easy to understand, there are certain jargons that you need to understand in order to operate in a better way. Here are some of the most common jargons used in affiliate marketing.

Advertiser

The advertiser is the person or company that produces the product or service. They are the ones who will affiliate with the Webmaster. They are better known as merchants in the world of affiliate marketing. These advertisers pay the Webmaster a commission for the number of people that buy their products thanks to the Webmaster's guidance.

Affiliate

The affiliate is the Webmaster who affiliates with the advertiser to promote his or her products. The advertiser for the number of clicks, leads or customers pays that he the affiliate or she brings in. The affiliate is also known as the web site owner.

Affiliate link

Affiliate links refer to URL addresses that are used to direct people to the merchant's website or products page. These links are present all over the website owner's page and clicking on them will take the user to the desired page owned by the merchant. These links are always unique, as the merchant needs to know who is to be credited for the traffic.

Affiliate program

The affiliate program is something that is used to track the number of clicks, leads etc. It is mostly used by the web master to keep track of how many people are clicking on the URL that is present on their website. The program is fully automatic and will give results instantly.

Banner ad

A banner ad refers to the merchant's electronic ad that is placed on the affiliate's website or blog page. It can be an animated banner, a gif, a JPEG image or mere writing. A banner ad generally appears on the top right corner of the page but can also be placed anywhere on the web master's page.

Click through

Click through refers to the process of the Webmaster's reader clicking on the merchant's URL and going to their website. It is referred to as a successful click through only if the reader visits the page and does not terminate it before he or she is redirected.

Commission

Commission refers to the income that the web master generates when he or she successfully creates a sale, lead or customer for the merchant. The merchant pays the affiliate a certain percentage of the sale and can also pay him or her fees.

Conversion rate

Conversion rate refers to the percentage of clicks that lead to a lead or a sale. The rate is used to calculate how much a particular Webmaster's website or blog is bringing in commissionable business to the merchant. It is also used to check the tie-ups efficiency for both the parties involved.

Cookies

Cookies refer to files that are sent to the reader or users web browser. The cookies are used to assign an identification to the user who has clicked on a particular affiliate's URL and accessed the merchant's product page or website. These cookies will remain in the user's browser for 30, 60 or more days depending on the website's policy. The user can return to the site at any time within that period and if he or she buys something then the affiliate is paid a commission.

Direct linking

Direct linking refers to the user directly accessing the merchant's website without being redirected. This proved to be convenient for the user and helps the affiliate with search engine rankings.

Disclosure

A disclosure is a message to the reader or user to know that you are an affiliate and are promoting goods and services of a merchant on your site. This disclosure can be placed anywhere on the page and is now a compulsion for all affiliates to have a disclosure on their site.

EPC

EPC stands for earnings per click. This refers to how much commission you earn per click. It is used to determine how much money is earned every time a reader or user clicks on the URL of the merchant. Now say for example you have earned $2000 for one year through your affiliation with a partner and 10000 clicks got you that money. Your earnings per click are calculated by dividing 2000 by 10000 that gives you 0.2, meaning you have earned 2 cents per click.

First click

The first click refers to the first source for the user to have found the merchant's product and has resulted in a successful purchase. The affiliate that was the source of the first click gets paid even if the user bought the product after clicking on another affiliate's link. That is, say X bought a product after clicking on Y's link but had already clicked on Z's link a while back. This works only if Z's cookies are still present in X's web browser.

Impression

An impression refers to the number times a particular ad is shown on the affiliate's web page. Each of the ads will count for one impression.

Last click

Last click refers to the last link that the user clicked before purchasing a product or service. This means that the advertiser pays the last source. The user's browser will have the first click's cookies and yet, the last click affiliate will be credited. That is, If X buys a product after clicking on Y's link then Y will be credited even if X had clicked Z's affiliate link. The presence of Z's cookies will not affect Y's earnings.

Lead

A lead can be the user's communication with the product's merchant. It can be a quote requested, a query posted or any other such thing. Most merchants specify the lead before going through with an affiliation.

Manual approval

When an affiliate applies for affiliation with an advertiser or advertising website then they can adopt one of two ways to check it. The first one being manual approval where personnel personally peruse the form and the second one being automatic where a computer program does the checking. Both are equally popular.

Niche

A niche refers to the web master's field of expertise and what his or her work is mainly based on. So if I were to write on gardening then my narrow niche would be gardening and agriculture would be my broader niche.

Pay per

Pay per is a term used to define what the affiliate is being paid based on. It can be pay per click- where they get paid for the number of click, pay per lead- where they get paid for the number of leads, pay per sale- where they get paid after every successful sale.

Raw clicks

Raw clicks refer to the number of clicks that an affiliate has received and will include the entire gamut of clicks even if the same person has clicked 20 or 30 times.

Recurring commission

Recurring commissions are paid when the reader or user repeatedly pays the merchant to receive a service. For example: if you redirect a reader to a magazine website where he or she has to pay on a monthly basis to receive the service then every time they pay the affiliate get paid a certain percentage.

Super affiliates

Initially, super affiliates was used a term to describe those who made $10,000 upwards by promoting others products and services but now, it is used to describe the top affiliates that help in generating the most sales for the merchant. It is believed that just the top 5% will help in bringing in 90% of the business.

Target marketing

Target marketing refers to selling products and services to a target audience. It is the responsibility of both the affiliate and the merchant to find the right product for the right customer at the right time in order to have a guaranteed sale.

Unique click

Unique clicks refer to the clicks that come from different sources and not multiple clicks from the same source. Merchants will only consider unique clicks before deciding on affiliating with an affiliate. The unique clicks are calculated by looking at the IP address and browser head of the clicker.

White labeling

White labeling refers to a merchant giving an affiliate to sell their products like it is their own. They will create an independent website for the affiliate and the user will not know that he or she is just an affiliate. This privilege is generally given to super affiliates.

Viral marketing

Viral marketing refers to the constant sale of products and services thanks to its popularity and word of mouth promotions. This will work best if the affiliate successfully convinces several people to click on the links of the products and services that they are promoting.

Some more terms

Affiliate Fraud: any activity that is designed by an affiliate with the intention of generating revenue illegally. This is done in a number of different ways like making use of fraudulently generated leads or clicks. Even a lot of affiliate set up fake accounts with the networks and even manage to generate through these accounts a lot of large value of transactions which are never paid for. They are simply betting that the merchant will not reverse the commissions generated in this particular manner.

Banner Ad: any graphic advertisement that has been displayed on the affiliate site

Charge Back: It is the same as reversals.

CTR: CTR stands for Click through rate or click through ratio. This is arrived at by dividing the total rate of clicks received by an ad by the number of impressions. So a simple illustration to make you understand this easily is; supposed an ad has been shown around a hundred times and it receives 20 clicks. Then the CTR would be 20%.

Click Reference: the facility that has been created by affiliates networks to offer unique links for tracking that are contained in a click reference. This allows the affiliates to identify the sales that have come through a specific page or a link that is present their site or any pay per click campaign.

CPA: CPA stands for Cost per Action. And in CPA payment in the form of commission is given out according to an action that can be recorded

CPC: CPC stands for Cost per click and the users make the payment according to the number of clicks on the affiliate link.

CPM: there are a number if affiliate programmes that pay on a CPM basis, which stands for Cost per impression.

CR: CR stands for Conversion rate or conversion ratio is achieved by adding up all the clicks obtained and dividing this sum by the number of sales that are generated.

Creative: These are similar to banner ads and are generally the graphic advertisements that are capable of being displayed on a site of an affiliate.

Cookieless Tracking: A lot web users these days are deleting or clearing off their cookies on a regular basis and even because of the concern over spyware programs that have come up, most of the networks have introduced a tracking program that is not based on the cookies generated.

Contextual Linking: in contextual linking the affiliate links designed for specific products are placed within the related information or even the articles present on a particular website.

Data Feed: the information of a product is usually contained in the data feed and this is a file that is generally in either CSV or XML format. This file contains the URL, name, image and description of a particular product being offered for sale. Many affiliates make use of these files to create content that would be relevant for their own site.

Drop Shipping: this is also a form of affiliate marketing. In data shipping there are two parties involved; an affiliate who is responsible for collecting orders and payment and the merchant who is responsible for delivering the product to the client directly. In this form of affiliate marketing there is no need for keeping a stock of goods or buying the goods at a wholesale price, and therefore the commission is slightly higher

Google Adsense: Google Adsense is an application developed by Google and this pays the website owners a certain amount of the cost per click whenever one of the ads that have been displayed has been clicked on.

Google Adwords: the Google search engine offers a pay per click solution. In this, advertisers pay according to CPC according to the type of content that is being offered by the site while also displaying the amount that other advertisers are willing to pay. Ads are displayed with the Google results.

Link Popularity: This represents the number of sites that are lining their site to yours and is also referred to as incoming links or backlinks.

Lifetime Commissions: same as the two tiers affiliate programme

Network Override: the additional charge along with the commission that has to be paid to the merchant by the networks is referred to as network override and the cost to payable to the merchant is usually 30%.

Merchant: either a business owner or an online retailer is referred to as a merchant.

PPC: PPC stands for Pay per Click and in this method of payment, the traffic generated towards a particular link is paid for according to the number of clicks it has received.

Residual Earnings: the income that is produced from those programmes wherein the merchants pay commission on the ensuing transactions generated by customers who have been referred by an affiliate.

Reversal: when the merchant himself removes or reduces sales commission due to an affiliate. This happens whenever there is any fraudulent activity or even when credit cards are declined.

Skyscraper: a skyscraper is a banner ad in the format o f120 X 600

SEO: SEO stands for Search engine optimisation and it is the process of making changes to an existing site to ensure that it is able to perform and achieve better results in the search engines.

Tiered Commission: the structure of commission that is being offered by the merchants and this increases on a sliding scale according to the performance.

Two Tier Affiliate Programme: this kind of a program usually reward an affiliate for signing on sub affiliates. For the entire duration that an affiliate lasts for, you also get a certain commission.

Chapter 17
Tips To Increase Your Income

When it comes to affiliate marketing, you need to consider increasing your commission. You cannot possibly remain in the same category for long and must aim higher. Here are some tips for you to do so.

Do you want to be an affiliate marketer? Have you just initiated the process of being an affiliate marketer? Affiliate marketing is an excellent way to not just generate an income online but also to monetize your websites. Your website could be about anything and everything, and affiliate marketing would help you make an earning out of it.

In this chapter you will learn about a simple yet very effective manner in which you can increase the income generated from affiliate marketing. Though most of the tips given in this chapter are for marketers who are making use of a paid traffic source like Google Adwords or even Facebook ads, the basic principles would hold true for traffic generated from any source, let it be original content or even viral marketing strategies.

It was mentioned earlier to not choose several affiliates as it can confuse the reader. But, if you use the affiliate links wisely and give them a few good options then chances of them clicking all links will be high. What's more is, they will decide between the choices and successfully place an order from one of the choices. So it pays to be wise with the decision of to employ 3 to 4 different merchants.

Make sure you put the compulsory disclosure to good use. You need to anyway declare that you have sprinkled affiliate ads all over your webpage so; it is best that you use it to coax people to click on the ads. Just make sure you don't come across as being needy of clicks or desperate for it and try and maintain a dignified way to tell people that you need the clicks to provide them with good, free content. You can make use of a hand written note to drive across a stronger message, as people will connect better if they see something that is personalized for them.

Sometimes, your links should be placed at obvious places and will automatically make people click on it. These places can be words that are hyperlinked or you say things like if you wish to buy this product then please click <u>here,</u> and hyperlink it. If you make it extremely confusing then your audience might not decipher it and you will lose out on potential commission. You will also get a low ranking on search engines for having secret links.

As soon as you realize your worth, don't refrain from asking for more commission. Ask the company to pay you better and if the profits they make thanks to you are staggering then consider threatening them by saying you are leaving.

Remember to make use of pop under ads to advertise your merchant's products and services. Remember that most of your readers will have software installed to prevent pop ups, which will render your affiliations useless. So make sure you choose pop under instead of pop ups.

If your blog is supremely popular and you are endorsing products of the best and premier brands then you can also do your own company's promotions. Say for example you own a site on baking and have a tie up with Pillsbury. You are promoting their cookie flour and dough and have your own brand for these as well. By mentioning both in the same breath you will increase your brand's value.

Once you have earned a good reputation and made enough profit, you can increase your website's worth by announcing prizes and gifts. This will help you have a sustained audience who will be interested in coming back to your page consistently. Make sure the prizes you offer are all interesting and well worth your reader's time. You can also get your affiliate merchant's to sponsor a few of the gifts and have their logo printed on it for publicity purposes.

Make the best use of the SEO tool to be noticed by bigwig merchants. If your blog or website happens to show up as the first result then you stand a good chance to get signed on by one of the best affiliate companies and increase your worth and profitability.

Make sure that you have an agreement to be paid for repeat sales. That is where most companies make maximum profit. A repeat customer is extremely valuable and if he or she was your find then it is best to ask the company for recurring commission. You can keep track of the customer and make sure that the company is not cheating you. You can also ask repeat customers to notify you so that you are not cheated.

Remember, it is up to you to increase your profits and make the most of the business. Your affiliate companies will not by themselves recognize your worth and you will have to bring it to their notice.

So, let us take a look at the seven ways in which you can increase your earning from affiliate marketing.

Tip#1

The first tip is that you should try different sources to generate traffic from. Whatever may be the product that you are promoting you will definitely need a lot of traffic and this traffic can be generated from various sources. So it is essential that you try the different sources of traffic before you zero in on any one of them. There are some offers that will prove to be more useful on Facebook whereas some others might be best suited for another source like a private media purchase. Whenever you come across any offer that looks very interesting, try considering the kind of buyer who is most likely to respond to that particular type of offer. You can make use of various tools available online to figure out the largest source of traffic for that offer. Let us suppose that one source of traffic for that particular offer is Facebook, and then it is highly probable that the offer would convert well on a social networking platform. Test as many sources that are capable of generating traffic before you lock in on one and see the best offers on return available for your ad spending too. If you think the sources of traffic are all going to be similar, then you are sadly mistaken. The difference between them could be extreme, it might be look like a brilliant offer on one site but when the same is transferred on to another site, it might turn out to be a complete dud.

Tip#2

The second tip is that you should make use of a landing page if you want to increase the rate of conversions. If you are able to send the traffic towards your offer without any deviations, then it should be more than enough to make a profit. But if you are looking for a means that you can make use of to increase your rate of conversions, then you should perhaps consider the idea of creating your own landing page and this landing page would act as the route that is necessary to bridge the gap between you ad and the offer to which you are sending the traffic. You need not worry about the complexity of landing pages. They need not be complicated, at all. In fact at time all you need is a clear and simple, easy to understand heading with all the key points written in highlighted font for you to increase your rate of conversion. With the right kind of design and good content your landing page would help in increasing your ROI manifold. And it is not that difficult to build your own landing page. With all the information that is available online, all it would take for you to come up with a decent enough landing page would be just some research. So get started on your research!

Tip#3

Did you know that you could ask your affiliate manager for a new and increased payout? Almost all of the CPA networks that are present, they work while having a margin of not less than 30%. So, let us translate this into simpler monetary terms. If you are earning around $30 per lead you get, then the affiliate network you make use of is earning for itself, anywhere from $7-$10 and this roughly accounts for 30% of your earnings. The affiliate networks earn a fixed commission for all the sales that you successfully make, and this is the reason why they prefer to have large volumes of conversions, rather than having several small campaigns that would help then get a high ROI. If you are able to generate a high number of leads, then you might be able to ask your affiliate manager to improve your payout to help improve the ROI you are generating.

Tip#4

Always track your campaigns. If you are not tracking your campaigns then you will seldom achieve profitability. There are a number of tracking applications and software that are readily available for the affiliates to make use of. Some of the popular choices are Proper202 and even CVP Lab. Before you start making use of any software or even an application, make sure that you done thorough research about it and you know all about the advantages and disadvantages they pose. Whether or not they have the feature to help you save and store your campaign data. You can either buy these or even make use of free trackers. There are free applications that can help you track your affiliate campaigns like Google analytics.

Tip#5

You can even design your own creatives for the purpose of advertising. The affiliate network you are making use of might provide you with readymade banners. Steer clear of these, these images might all look good but then these aren't designed with the intention of obtaining a good conversion rate. You needn't make use of banners designed by professional. Often at times opting for the simplest of creatives can be more effective. At times even the banners with large eye catching titles prove to be more effective. If you want to make your campaign successful then you might have to test a lot of banners, anywhere from around 5 banners to 500 banners.

Tip#6

Try testing similar offers that are available. Let us take for instance some of the most popular affiliate marketing niches. Gaming and dating seem to be the two fields in which there are thousands of different offers available for you to promote. In such a field, you will notice that having an ad campaign that is more effective will make all the difference. Since the offers available are so similar, an effective ad campaign for any one of them can result in a completely diverse CPA offer. If you have designed an ad campaign that is generic that is capable of being used for any offer available in the chosen niche, then you can test it on a number of CPA offers to see which one of these would provide the best ROI.

Tip#7

To increase not just your earnings but also the ROI, you can start scaling profitable existing campaigns and even new traffic sources like Facebook. It is true that the affiliate campaigns do not last forever, and most of the profitable campaigns are usually spotted before they are able to fully get into their target market by other affiliates. So, you will have to start scaling to find a winning campaign.

Chapter 18
Types of Affiliate Marketing

Let us now look at the three types of affiliate marketing that you can choose between.

Unattached affiliate marketing

This is the first and possibly the most popular form of affiliate marketing. Here, there is no need for the person to have an authority over the niche. So the person will only sprinkle the links of the affiliate and hope for the reader to click on them and earn a commission for it.

Some purists are against this concept and don't think of it as a good business models. They are of the opinion that not having authority over the niche market does not give the person the right to promote products and services. It is too vague for them to do so and should not cut into the profits.

However, not having to slog over finding a large audience base makes this type extremely popular amongst several people. The person does not have to have a strong online presence and can only be someone who accesses the Internet regularly.

This pay per click concept is preferred by all those who are looking to make a quick buck and not really interested in making affiliate marketing their parallel source of income for life.

You can consider this type if you are looking for quick affiliate marketing fix. If you like the business and wish to make it a full time source of income then you can shift to another type.

You can sign up with affiliate marketing programs to get started on this type and you can get started in no time.

Related affiliate marketing

Related affiliate marketing is the next type of affiliate marketing that you can choose for yourself. This type is unlike the previous one where you do not need any online presence to indulge in affiliate marketing. Here, you will need a strong online presence in order to affiliate with companies.

But the products and services that you endorse might not be directly related to your content or you might not use them yourself and are merely promoting them.

So you do not have the added responsibility of vouching for a product's worth and can merely promote it to your readers and users.

Now say for example you have a blog for fashion footwear. You can promote in soles that will help people remain comfortable. Now you might not yourself use these particular insoles but have used insoles in the past.

This type will account for related affiliate marketing. You do not have to feel for the product and can only refer it as an example to your readers.

You can consider moving to this type after having tried the previous method. You can also have both, as there is no limit to the types of affiliate marketing that you can take up at once.

Involved affiliate marketing

The third type is known as involved affiliate marketing. This is probably the best type to adopt if you are really interested in making affiliate marketing your ticket to success.

Involved affiliate marketing refers to immersing yourself into the marketing process as much as possible. So, you need to believe in the products and services that you are endorsing and must promote them honestly.

You can choose the products that you swear by. It can be a cosmetics brand, a fashion brand or a sports brand that sells tennis rackets. As long as you use the products yourself and are interested and spreading the good word, you will rake in a big profit.

Remember that you have to add in personal experiences in order for people to trust you. There is a need for your readers to connect with you and the products alike.

The more that you harp about the products or service's goodness, the more the word of mouth and the better the sales

When you decide to personally involve yourself with something you will have the chance to become a super affiliate that means that you will unlock several privileges.

Once you establish yourself as a bona fide involved affiliate marketer, there will be no turning back and you will have a chance to reap in elevated profits.

Some more types of affiliate marketing

Affiliate marketing often allows for not just the growth but also the creation of different types of affiliates. The experience that you have gathered from PPC advertising or even from the creation of original content for various sites, blogs and forums or even the large circle of acquaintances and friends on all the social networking sites. Whatever knowledge you have gathered from any of the different aspects of your life can be put to use and help in converting the Internet traffic into income by making the use of affiliate marketing.

Till now you have looked at some types of affiliate marketing. Following are some more types of affiliate marketing:

Content sites

Content sites include blogs, websites or even catalogues, all such sites that have got content in them just like their name suggests. Affiliates that fall in this category make use of such content sites and cash in on the sites traffic by sending the users of this site pages of advertiser through text links or even ad banners. These sites can be of two types. They can either be general or specific in nature. A general site then the volume of traffic recorded them would be on the higher side since they serve the public in general. The second type is a niche site, these sites would target only a select audience and therefore the traffic turnover would be slightly less, but then again, their conversion rate would be more than a general site.

A PPC affiliate

PPC affiliate would someone who can put the experience gained by them in PPC advertising to some good use create a link. In such a case, they would directly send the users of the site to the website of the advertiser. To put it simply, someone making use of a ppc affiliate would not have a website of their own. This kind of affiliate marketing is considered to have a high risk factor because the affiliate would pay according to the number of clicks they receive from the users but they would only receive their payment from the network they are a part of once the click has been transformed into a sale or a lead that has been completed.

Making use of emails and newsletters

These are such affiliates who have databases filled with information about the users and they make use of such information to send out not just offers but even various suggestions through the medium of newsletters. As it would be while making use of any means of communication it is essential to ensure that there is some regulation followed. It must be made sure that the email addresses have been gathered legally and the users themselves have voluntarily and willing requested for the various emails they are receiving from the affiliate. The newsletters send out often contain promotions and various offers.

Making use of social media

Social media is on an upswing and it does not look like it will ever slow down. Popular social networking sites such as Facebook, twitter and so on; have facilitated in the creation of a new type of an affiliate program altogether, an affiliate who would send users through his or her own account on these social networking websites. The affiliates who fall under this category do not rely on the users of their sites, instead they rely on their own circle of friends, acquaintances and even followers they have acquired on the carious social networking platforms.

Services provided for shopping

The affiliates who fall under this category include all those websites that have been built while keeping in mind a specific service that would facilitate in the promotion of online purchases. Some of the most common examples of these sites are websites that offer price comparison, review sites and even aggregators. The actual manner in which these sites monetize their value is on the basis of their content, because these sites help in redirecting the users towards the sites of retailers in order for them to complete their purchase.

Traffic that has been incentivized

This form of affiliate marketing can be best described as the sort wherein the visitors to these sites have been given a compensation of sort for visiting the site and then completing a specific action. The compensation they are given is in monetary terms usually or it can also be virtual currency. Affiliates receive a commission from the network which they later on split with the users.

Chapter 19

The Best Ways to Start with Affiliate Marketing

There are many different ways on how to get started with affiliate marketing. However, the best way is to invest and to enroll in high quality courses or programs that can teach people how to do affiliate marketing. Courses that may help you get started with affiliate marketing are:

- Niche Profit Classroom

- Niche Profit Course

- Chris Farrell Membership

- Internet Business Mastery

These courses will teach you about the general Internet marketing techniques and will go through affiliate marketing as well. Learning things by yourself is also an option but is not highly advisable. If you invest some money in learning to do things the right way, it will save you much time and at the same time, will avoid going through many failures.

There are also some investment costs in affiliate marketing as well as some software and tools. Below are the list of resources recommending in set up your blog and start making money with affiliate marketing.

GoDaddy

The world's No. 1 domain name registration service provider.

BlueHost

A hosting website which is easy to use, provides a one-click automatic WordPress installation and excellent customer service.

WordPress

A free blogging platform that is fully customizable and has a wonderful support system.

Market Samurai

The best tool for keyword research which will assist you in discovering what website to get into and does all the research needed to be successful.

Unique Article Wizard

One of the best article submission and article marketing service that can create back links to your blog and assist in increasing your search engine ranking.

Google Analystics

A free website analystic and tracking tool by Google which allows the blog owner access to all the stats and activities going in the blog site.

AWeber

The best emails opt-in and marketing tool that will assist you in building your email listing and newsletter.

Andy Anderson

Chapter 20

Various Niches and Their Profitability

One of the biggest questions that all the affiliates ask is about the different niches that are available to them and the profitability of these niches. In this chapter we will answer this question and it will also help you decide about the kind of niche you are interested in.

The evergreen niches are those niches whose need and popularity will never reduce. There are some markets that never go out of trend and are always possible. There are three evergreen niches that you can consider and these are health, wealth and love/romance

Health market would include niches related to various topics like weight reduction, different diets, medical issues related to it and also lifestyle tips. So if you consider yourself to be a fitness fanatic or even a lifestyle expert then this is the best suitable niche for you.

Wealth, well who doesn't want to be able to create more if it? This would include Internet marketing, foreign exchange management and even gambling to some extent. Anything and everything can be useful in the generation of wealth would be included in this.

The third evergreen niche refers to anything that has got to do with love. Like online dating sites, marriage registrars, social networking sites, or even hacks for getting back with your ex, finding a life partner and so on.

All of the above mentioned are major markets and will never go out of fashion. You should not just explore more about these major markets but also the sub niches related with this topic. You can count on banking on the curiosity and in some cases even desperation showed by individuals. More often than not, it so happens that customers are looking for an easy way out. They want to be able to achieve the results without putting in any effort, so this is when you can promote your own product. Affiliate marketing is an endless loop and there will be many opportunities that will seem profitable.

- Hobbies and activities

Hobbies and related activities never go out of business. For you to be able to cash in on this, you will have to select a particular type of a hobby idea that a lot of people would be willing to spend money on. You need to find something that makes people happy and they would want to come back to it again. When you are thinking of hobbies and related activities, think big. Think along the lines of expensive hobbies like golfing, sailing, travelling and even hunting. These are the kind of activities that people involved will have to spend a lot of money on. They will need to buy new equipment and tools to continue their hobby. People would be willing to splurge on guides and even instructors to help them with this. The product you promote need not be a physical product, it can even be digital. There are a variety of sub niches related to this, you should explore them too to promote.

- Affiliate products and services with a high payout

There are some affiliate products that have a high payout when compared to the rest. The products and services offered would include loans, online casinos, and a variety of luxury goods like watches, handbags and jewelry. Anything that has a ring of luxury to it, would be a good bet to explore. It does not take any extra effort to promote a luxury product. It would probably take as much time to promote a normal eBook as it would to promote a luxury handbag. In this case, the volume of sales need not be high for you to be able to make a big fat commission. The rate of refund on high end products is usually less too. No individual would make a rash decision while spending on a luxury product so if they indeed are buying something, then they would have thought things through. And generally, it is an assumption that those who are able to and can also afford to buy luxury products have an ample of money. So it would be safe to call these niches as recession proof.

For instance, take the example of a payday loan. There never is any shortage of the number of people who would want a loan to meet their requirement, and it is safe to say that once an individual has taken a loan, then it is highly likely that the said individual will opt for a loan again. However cold this might sound, but poverty is a vicious cycle, and once any person gets stuck in it, they usually stay in it. That's what happens with borrowings too. Gambling is addictive, and those who gamble on a regular basis cannot stop gambling. And are always on the lookout for new casinos. This is a brilliant idea to invest in. gambling never goes out business even during terrible economic conditions. Most of the casinos also pay the affiliate a certain portion of the money that the casino has gained from a player.

If you are looking for a niche that helps you make money, then you should consider one of the above niches. But if it isn't something that you are passionate about, there are millions other ideas you can always invest in. the above-mentioned are highly lucrative, profitable and also attract a huge number of customers.

In conclusion I would just like to say that the niches of health, wealth and money would never be out of business. Because people always have problems with these three aspects and they would not mind spending money on having them solved instead of trying to put in some hard work and solve it themselves. People would never give up on their hobbies that make them happy, and such individuals will not mind spending on being happy. Those who are obsessed with the world of fashion would not mind splurging on the latest fashion accessories. There is as such no niche that can top the lists as being the most profitable one. But there are some strong contenders for that title. The above-mentioned niches will help you earn a huge commission, because the demand for products or services offered in them has not decreased, and it will keep increasing. So chose your niche wisely.

Chapter 21
How to Select a Profitable Niche

Although it is a celebrated fact that Affiliate marketing is the most efficient way to earn money but the assumption is skeptical as product quality plays a vital role for the consumers to accept and own it for their needs.

Competition in today's industry is the key factor for any product to survive. The manufacturer should fight this with a well-defined strategy and enter the area with a goal i.e. minimal competition and maximum revenue. The art of exploring a profitable niche for affiliate marketing should be the primary agenda.

Promoting the right niche on the right platform could be a challenging task but this could be achieved by following basic principles.

These principles involve selecting the domain name with fewer characters and the hypothesis that longer domain name leads to better rank is a myth.

The first step w.r.t. Affiliate marketing is to key in a topic in Google keyword planner tool and estimate the monthly searches rather than following a laborious pattern of creating lot of content.

Considering that one might find words that have many search patterns, considering them would not be a great idea, as the competitors would have already used it. These could be few tactics to stay away from the competitive world and focus on a sub niche for which very minimal searches on Google.

The next strategy would be considering the niche that would generate revenue, creating an informational content might not be a great idea.

The usual buyers are generally interested in searching for reviews, pictures and videos of using the products, as they are not looking learning about the product but then to buy it.

Bearing in mind that for a particular product the search results on Google are not too popular but then if the number of searches are significant then this conveys that people are really interested in that product. This could be the most efficient way to understand the consumer's needs by creating content and adding the necessary affiliate links. Although this strategy could be key, it should be carefully handled as the consumers should not search for information and leave the website. To solve this use review models and videos.

So when the above steps of having a niche, browsing the best affiliate network and some positive search from Google keyword planner tool the step way forward is to find the right product to promote for the niche.

Recommending the products that have been tried would be a game changer as this would significantly help in promoting and creates awareness in identifying the scammers.

Each niche could be divided into thousands of sub niches so limiting it would not be a great idea might complicate things. Best niches are the ones that generate a lot of money and software products.

Games and dating could be few examples of the successful niches to be promoted as marketers make thousands of dollars per day. While coming to dating it could be a high traffic site and for topics related to relationship making it an easy conversion.

Another example would be the computer and electronic world to promote since it is a good niche.

Web hosting is also considered to be a very profitable niche and this could be divided into several sub – niches and in turn have services to promote and scale up. For hosting every service they would pay 200$ and that is very high commission and very few follow the same. The most exciting part is the program part that is a premium hosting service that could be promoted and be proud of.

All the principles considered above should be considered with a great focus, steps such as finding a profitable niche, creating a content that has very minimal search results and high customer views and which also could indirectly increase in customer buying the product and not just for fun should be followed judiciously

Promoting general niches that are being promoted by popular blogs should not be considered as it involves a lot of industry competition. The product that is being promoted should have the stability to undergo different phases of the product life cycle to be established and to be successful in the market. Focusing on specific niche and promoting the right product could be the way going forward to achieve profit via affiliate marketing

Chapter 22
Affiliate Marketing through Blogging

What is Blogging?

Blogging, an act of posting contents on a blog or online journal, is very popular nowadays. It also became a popular SEO or Search Engine Optimization.

A blog, sometimes also called as weblog, is an informational site or a discussion published on the Internet. Jorn Barger used the term weblog on December 17, 1997. Peter Merholz initially used the short term of weblog, which is blog, for his blog site, Peterme.com in May 1999. Pyra Labs and Evan Williams used the term "blog" as a noun and as a verb, meaning to add content to a blog or to maintain. Labs and Williams derived with the term blogger, in connection with the Blogger product of Pyra Lab.

Before blogs became popular, a lot of people and even companies make use of different mediums like Usenet, Bulletin Board Systems, and email lists. By the year 1990, an Internet Forum Software company that connects messages on a virtual corkboard created threads or running conversation.

Nowadays, blogging is used by a lot of people as an online diary, where the blog author can keep a running account of his personal life. A blog is consisted of posts or entries of the blog owner, displayed in reverse chronological order, where the most recent post appears first. Combination of text, pictures, links, web pages, and videos can be transmitted from the author's personal computer to his blog site.

Aside from an individual user, multi-users can also maintain blogs, where different authors from different businesses and organizations can write the posts. Multi-author blogs are from newspapers, universities, advocacy groups, real estate companies and other institutions. A lot of blogs function not only as a personal online diary but also as a brand advertising of an individual or a company. A lot of bloggers are using their blogs to introduce arts, videos, photographs, music and audio to advertise their works and eventually sell them. Nowadays, a lot of bloggers are using their blogs not only to advertise and sell their own products but also to advertise other people and company and eventually make profit out of it.

Andy Anderson

Chapter 23
Benefits of Keeping a Blog

We are now living in a digital age where information exists and accessible at the tips of our fingers. Most people around the globe to get information delivered fast can use Internet.

Regardless of what industry a person or a company came from, whether it is from education, financial service, real estate or media, one of the most effective and efficient ways to provide information to prospects and customers is to have and maintain a blog. Here are the reasons why utilizing the power of blogging will help your organization and business grow:

1. Prospects and potential customers can find you easily.

   Every time you post valuable and relevant information on your blog, it will give the major search engines like Google and Yahoo more incentives for your articles to be on the Search Engine Optimization (SEO) or to be on top of the search results. The more information you keep in your blog, the more likely that your blog will appear as top research result for your prospects.

Giving your prospects and potential customers an easier way to find you is very powerful. Instead of calling your prospects, who may or may not be interested in what you are offering or selling, these people will be the ones to look for you when they are looking for products and services they are seeking.

2. Your competitors may not have a blog of their own.

    Creating a blog is sharing information about yourself, your business, as well as your products and services which will give you a more competitive advantage. Even though most companies and professionals still depend on phone calls and face-to-face interactions, this method is effective in establishing your business' presence online. Establishing a strong online presence will help you to stand out among hundreds, or even thousands of competitors serving the same market.

3. You can engage more with your potential customers.

Interacting with existing and possible customers using a blog is an excellent medium. Giving the readers an opportunity to provide feedbacks and suggestions as well as asking questions will assist you not only in addressing each person's concerns but also to demonstrate that as a business owner, you care enough for them by communicating with them. This will build the trust and likeability of each client to do business with you again. You will also build an authority as a business owner who writes helpful and professional articles. This will establish your credibility as a source of information, as well as one of the top leaders of your industry.

4. Many doors may open for you.

One of the greatest benefits of blogging is the countless opportunities that will come to you because you have a blog. A lot of individuals have received job offers, promotional offerings and even asked to speak in different conferences and events and this will not be impossible to happen to you too.

Always keep in mind that not only potential customers may visit your blog but also other professionals not only from your industry but also outside as well. Fruitful opportunities that may open to you are endless.

Chapter 24

Strategies in Making Income from Your Blog

1. Build your email listing.

   By the time that you launch your blog, give time to build your email listing too. Your blog will not be a profitable business if you don't have a list of subscribers and potential customers.

   Tips for building your email list:

   - In exchange for joining your email listing, offer some incentives like an e-book or training video, for free.

   - Do not just collect email addresses; get the names of the owners too.

- Use different methods in capturing your leads. Put an option box in your blog's sidebar or generate a pop up where people may be directed to your page.

2. Build a lasting relationship with your subscribers.

A lot of bloggers believe that the bigger your email listing is, the more money you will be able to make. This is generally true; however, your relationship with your blog's email listing is far more important. A good and lasting relationship with 500 subscribers is more worthy than having a bad relationship with 5,000 or more subscribers. Always remember that the success of a blog depends on the supporters and not just with the contents or value of the channel.

Provide your subscribers with value: know who your subscribers are, what their problems are all about and provide them all the information they need to solve those problems. One of the ways to provide consistent value to your subscribers is to send a series of email by the use of email marketing software. You may be able to send a broadcast message to your email list whenever you want, anytime you want.

3. Establish your credibility.

You must be separated from everyone else. Establish your credibility not only as a blogger but as an expert in your chosen field.

Here are some ways to begin in positioning yourself as an expert of your   field:

- Have an interesting story to tell.

- Speak at a conference or event.

- Have an individual interview you.

- Get professional photos of you taken.

- Get photos of you next to another expert or celebrity.

- Make a video of yourself speaking about an interesting topic and post it in your website.

- Write a book – it's your ultimate business card.

There are no secret strategies for every expert to reach what they are now, only fundamentals. The reasons why a lot of bloggers are now successful are because they have mastered not only the fundamentals of blogging but because they have built an online business as well. Always keep in mind that there is no shortcut to success. Learning the fundamentals and paying your due will help you reap your rewards at the end.

Here are some final tips to grow as a blogger:

- Always deliver value and be consistent.

- Don't be a do-it-yourself person. Get help if you needed.

- Don't treat your blog as a hobby, treat it as a business.

- Have fun. Don't take things too seriously.

Chapter 25

The Best Ways to Start With Blogging

One of the best sites for hosting your blog is by the use of Bluehost. Bluehost is a hosting software, which is required for you to host your blogs who can give you a free domain name when you use them. Bluehost is user friendly. Here are the ways on how to create your own blog and be able to set it up in minutes.

Step 1. Visiting the Bluehost website.

Singing up with Bluehost is easy and they offer an "Anytime Guarantee," which means if you don't want their service anymore and you want to cancel, you can do that any time and you will be able to get a refund of the amount that you paid for that wasn't used for hosting.

Step 2. Add your domain name.

You will be asked by the website to provide your domain name. The domain name will be the URL for your blog that people will use when visiting your blog. Make sure that the domain name you want is available and not yet taken. Make sure as well that the domain name that you will be using is easy to remember and can easily catch the attention of anyone surfing the Internet.

Step 3. **Enter your basic information and choose your package.**

You must fill up your personal information in the form that Bluehost will be providing and at the same time, you must select the hosting package that you want to avail. You will also enter your payment information at this point before you can proceed in setting up your actual blog. Most recommended for those starting a blog is to use the 12-month package.

Step 4. **Setup a Password and Login**

Create a password for your Bluehost login so that you can have a secure account. Once you create your password, you will be asked to login again using either your username and domain name and password and you will be directed to your control panel.

Step 5. **Click the Website Tab and select your platform**

Click the Website tab once you are logged in and you will be provided with a list of platforms to use; most recommended is

WordPress. You can then link your WordPress account with what you have set up with Bluehost and you'll be on your way to publish your own blog.

Once you have set up your blog, there are still a few things to remember before you publish your blog:

- Setup a theme for your blog. Make sure it is easy to navigate. It should also be easy on the eyes as well in terms of the color scheme of your choice.

- Install plug-ins to your blog. Plug-ins is another way for you to customize your blog. If you use WordPress, a list of available plug-ins can be found there.

- Try to install an application that will track your visitors. A recommended application will be Google Analytics.

- Start posting your content, and you can set up an "About" post to introduce yourself. The sooner you post high-quality content into your blog, the sooner you will be able to get visitors.

Andy Anderson

Chapter 26
Affiliate Marketing through Podcasting

Podcasts can also be used as a means of advertising and affiliate marketing. If you are running a blog, you can broadcast your blog content by uploading a podcast every now and then for your followers to listen to. Affiliate marketing can be done here so if you are to mention a brand that you have a contract with, you'll be advertising them and you'll be paid for that as well.

What is Podcasting?

Some may have an opinion regarding certain matters and some just want to talk. In doing so, being able to broadcast what they want can have different forms. With the help of the Internet, you will only need a computer, a fast Internet connection and special software to do so, and you can create a podcast.

A podcast is a set of files, typically an audio file that is subscribed to by followers and can be downloaded so that it can be listened to from a computer or a portable media player. The podcast was first known as "audioblogging" and it's been done from as early as the 1980's. The popularity of audioblogging only picked up when fast Internet connections became available and portable media players became more affordable.

The word "podcast" was coined from the combination of two words: the word "broadcast," and since most podcasts are played from portable media players, the term "pod" is used coming from the iPod media player.

Ben Hammersley first used the word podcast in The Guardian newspaper way back February 2004. During that time, they were trying to create a name for a new medium for broadcasting. There are also other names for podcasting, with the next popular being "netcasting." This term was coined to try to remove the association of podcasting to the iPod brand.

Nowadays, podcasts are very popular and is also commonly used to hear out opinions from known bloggers, celebrities and such. They can be downloaded into media players and then can be listened to whenever they want. Unlike online streaming where you will need a constant Internet connection to continue listening, podcasts are saved into your computer or player. Recently, podcasts with videos are becoming available from some podcast hosts like Apple. These are nicknamed "vodcasts" or "vidcasts" and they contain both audio and video content.

It's not just an individual who can create a podcast; groups and organizations can create a podcast for their own benefit too. Audio books are available as podcasts and some newspapers had taken advantage of this so they can create a podcast version of their newspaper content.

Andy Anderson

Chapter 27

Benefits of Starting and Keeping a Podcast

Setting up a podcast has a lot of advantages. With everyone being on the go nowadays, there are only few who will take time to sit down and read something from the Internet, whether it is news, an opinion, a radio show or whatnot. Some other advantages and benefits in keeping a podcast are:

Preparing a podcast is easier and faster than setting up a video.

You will just need your voice and something to talk about. Some may not be too comfortable in speaking in front of a camera, but has a lot of things to say, so a podcast can be the best choice.

Creating a podcast will help in sending out what you feel to those who may be listening.

Unlike written words, people will be able to hear your voice and your emotions through podcasting and with that, they will be able to feel what you are feeling personally. It is a means of connecting to your target audience.

Hearing is better than reading.

Hearing words rather than reading them is an easier way for people to "digest" what you want to say. Instead of sitting down and reading, you can multitask while listening to a podcast.

It kills time, the more productive way.

Bloggers can easily take a timeout from writing and they can set up a podcast every now and then. Doing a podcast will still allow you to make your brainwork, but unlike other things like writing, speaking can be done impromptu and it makes listening enjoyable in a sense.

It is easier and faster to set up a podcast.

Unlike making a video where you may need advanced equipment to record quality videos, setting up a podcast can be as simple as getting a microphone and an audio editing software. Editing and uploading podcasts is relatively easier and faster compared to setting up a video and rendering it.

Chapter 28

Strategies in Earning Money through Affiliate Marketing from Podcasting

Setting up podcasts will allow a lot of possibilities to get to you, and we can add the fact that you can become a new rising celebrity because of it as well. To be able to do that, reaching your target audience is important, and there are a few things that must be remembered:

Find and Identify Your Target Avatar

You must be able to know who you will be talking to. If you are to create a podcast, but in it you have no one to "talk to," then no one will "listen" to you.

Give a Definite Theme

Once you have an idea of who your avatar is, you must then get to your niche. A podcast with no sense of a theme is also going to be useless; no one will listen to it, which will put all your efforts to waste.

Provide the Best Content with Your Podcast

Once your audience knows that your podcasts are consistent and entertaining, you can start building on it. Make sure you have the richest content possible and that everything that goes into your podcast is consistent.

Promote it

Once you have the audience going, you may want to try to broaden your horizon, so to speak. Promoting your podcast will be the way to go. Encourage those that are not yet aware of your podcast to try listening, and see if they will come back for more.

Now once your podcast has become popular, sponsors may start approaching you. It is not necessary for the sponsors to go to you immediately; it may take a few weeks or months, depending on how popular your podcasts become.

Once the sponsors have taken notice of you, they will then try to negotiate and set up a deal with you. The usual deal may be with what they would call the "Industry Standard."

The Industry Standard has two parts:

- **15-second Pre-Roll:** This is when the host mentions the product or service of the sponsor for 15 seconds. This happens before the actual podcast starts.

- **60-second Mid-Roll:** This is when the host can talk about his sponsor's product or service within the middle of the podcast for 60 seconds. This is usually done around halfway of the podcast, around 40% to 70% within the show.

There may be cases as well where the host may mention his sponsors during his podcast's "outro," or the closing sequences, which is the time when the host will be giving his closing remarks, or after the closing remarks are done.

With the Industry Standard, a 15-second pre-roll may go at around $18 per 1000 listens, and the 60-second mid-roll may go at around $25 per 1000 listens.

There may be cases that the sponsors will approach you first, but you may also try going to sponsors yourself. You must make sure as well that when you get sponsors, they should go along with your niche. It will then be easy to create the pre-rolls and mid-rolls if your podcast sponsors are related to the topics that you have. Try to get a sponsor that you also trust; it will be hard to make a pre-roll or mid-roll for a product or service that you do not trust. Make sure as well that when making a deal with sponsors, be careful with the numbers and try to go with the minimum first. A sponsor may turn you down if you start to demand too much.

Chapter 29
The Best Ways to Start with Podcasting

Podcasting, known as the radio show of the new generation, is a combination of the words iPod and broadcasting. It involves computers, laptops, portable music players and almost any gadgets that can be connected to the internet.

Planning to start a podcast can be fun, but unless careful planning is done, your efforts may go to waste. Before you start hosting your own podcast for a single event or series, prepare first all the things that you will need during your recording.

- Software for audio recording

- Software for video editing

- Website or blog to publish your recording

- Sound effects or music (optional)

A few pointers can also be given so that you can then start you way on creating a successful podcast:

1. Setup a Topic

   In creating a podcast, you must first think of the product, or niche, that you will want to "sell," and you must also think of your target audience or avatar. Creating a podcast with an inconsistent topic may discourage current and first –time listeners and you may lose your audience as fast as how you can get them.

2. Give your Podcast a Name

   A name must be given to your podcast so that listeners can identify you easily. The trick is that the name should be easily remembered, it should be related to your topic and you must think of your niche and avatar as well; it should be related to your niche and that your avatar should be able to remember it quickly.

3. Create a Website for Your Podcast

   Try to set up a "home base" for your podcast by creating a website. This will serve as the place where your audience can go to so they can check more about your podcast or check for more information about you.

4. Setup a Format

This has to be consistent because this is what your audience will be expecting when they listen to your podcast. You have to set up the length of your podcast; too short may make the podcast uninteresting and too long may make it boring. The consistency of your topics should be there as well and be consistent with the release of the podcasts if you are going to do it on a regular basis.

5. Setup Your Equipment

A USB microphone and audio recording and editing software will be what you'll need to record and prepare a podcast. These can be fairly cheap and some of the software for recording and editing may be available for free as well.

With all of these steps, you'll be on your way to create your podcasts.

Andy Anderson

Chapter 30
Affiliate Marketing through Information Marketing

What is Information Marketing?

In this day and age, information is important. Owning information about certain things is as valuable as having a physical item, and selling that can become profitable for most. Selling such an important commodity and earning well from it is called information marketing.

The concept of information marketing has been around for a long time. Information that you will need can be given to you in exchange for information that you can give back. With information marketing, the information that you are selling can be of anything and it can be sold through different types of media. Newspapers, books, radio and TV are some of the types of media that you can use, but the easiest way to get into information marketing is using the Internet.

Using the Internet as a tool for selling information can be quick and easy. Setting up a blog about your favorite topic is one way and broadcasting a podcast on a regular basis is another way. Those who will read your blog or listen to your podcast will be given some information and in turn, they may either give a hit to your site or buy your information.

An e-book is also another way for you to get into information marketing. E-books and blogs are what they call "information products." These are what your target audience will be looking for and what they will buy from you.

Getting into information marketing is relatively easy. You will need to make sure that your information about a product is of high quality, and you also need to make sure you know how to sell it.

There are a lot of advantages and benefits with getting into information marketing. One big advantage is that all of your work can be done at the comforts of your own home. You will just need yourself to start working on giving information about a product, and you will not need any special education to start one. You can begin by writing something that you like or something that you are good at, and you want to have this information sent out to your target audience. You must know who your audience is and how to approach them.

Once you get the hang of information marketing, you can then sit back and let the market do the work for you.

Andy Anderson

Chapter 31
Benefits of Getting into Information Marketing

If you are able to play everything correctly with information marketing, earning money will be easy. Aside from the fact that you can just do this from your own home, getting into information marketing has its own advantages:

1. Leveraging What You Know

    This can be compared to how you work for someone and you get paid for what you do. Once you stop, you also stop getting paid. With information marketing, all you will need to do is produce a product and sell it. As long as your product keeps selling, you will be able to earn money, even if you stopped what you are doing.

2. Buyers Will Want to Buy More of Your Product

Once you have your target niche reading your information product, they will start wanting to get more information from you. They may end up "hiring" you for consultation regarding the things that you have written. They may also try to buy other information products that you may have or they may even try to get other products that you recommend. This ensures that you are turned into the "expert" on the subject.

3. Very Minimal Buyer Contact

All the transactions with information marketing are done online. Very minimal or no physical interaction with your buyer can occur. This also opens the big opportunity that everyone wants to do: being able to work at home. If you can continue producing information products, regardless of where you are located, you'll be sure to get buyers that will look for and buy your product.

4. Minimal Working Staff

In the information marketing business, minimal number of staff working for you can be possible. It is also possible that you alone can manage your business, but it can be helpful if you are to outsource some of your tasks with an independent party. This makes sure you have a better control over what is happening with your information product and how your business is running.

5. Starting From a Small Investment

Once you identify your niche and you have your information product, you can start selling it, and selling it doesn't need you to shell out a lot of cash. Being able to publish and sell your information product may still require you to invest a small amount of money, but all you will generally need is a way for you to create the product that your audience is looking for, publish it easily and make your audience want to get it. As long as you are confident and the information product that you are selling has high-quality content, selling it will be easy.

6. Earning Big is Possible

In every business, earning money does not happen overnight. Same goes for information marketing. You cannot expect your product to sell immediately after you publish it. Marketing and promoting it so that your niche can find out about it is the way for you to start selling. It will also help if you can get positive reviews about your products and continuous selling will ensure that you will continue to earn more. You may try to raise your price, as long as your content will still be of high quality.

Chapter 32

How to Get Started with Information Marketing

There are a number of steps to take to get into information marketing. These would be tedious but in the long run, it will be fruitful for you and you will start to see money rolling in. Remembering these steps will ensure that you can get a good start with information marketing:

1. Find Your Market

    You must first think of who you will be targeting with the information that you will be selling. Your theme or niche must be thought of thoroughly in order for you to have something to sell.

2. Think of a Good Title

Having a good title to work with is important; if your title is not catchy or not easy to remember, your target market will not catch on with what you are selling. Your title must be properly related to your niche, and the title should be able to tell anyone what they can expect when they read your information.

3. Choose Your Media for Your Information

Selecting your way of giving out the information is important. Through the Internet, there are two popular ways to do this; write a blog, or write an e-book.

In writing a blog, there are a few things that need to be mentioned:

- Buy the domain for your blog. This will make sure that your blog will only carry your name and the site will be easy to visit.

- Write high-quality contents and have keywords optimized so that people searching for information can find it easily.

- Once you get a few visits, try to set up an opt-in page so that you can see those who are following you. Try to give more contents for those who sign up.

- Set up a survey every now and then so that you'll know what your audience wants to see from you in the future.

Writing an e-book will have a similar scenario, but writing one will have a different approach:

- In writing an e-book, you can just make it as long as 20 to 30 pages and make a series that may be sell at a cheap price.

- Make sure you can get a cover that will stand out and catch a buyer's attention.

- Publish your e-book. One way to publish it is with Kindle; you will need to set up a Kindle Direct Publishing account and then format your e-book to match with what Kindle recommends. Publishing may take up to 24 hours after submitting it.

- Have your e-book ranked for your keywords. You may also want to have your e-book reviewed. Kindle also have a means to assist you in promoting your e-book.

Once you are able to establish your blog or e-book, you may also take advantage of a few things like hiring a virtual assistant and be consistent with the niche that you are into. Writing more content for your blog or e-book may have you do it or you can have it outsourced as well.

You can also do both blogging and writing an e-book. You can use your blog to promote your e-book, create a promotion and then launch your product. Give offers along with your product so that your audience will be encouraged to buy it.

Making money go around with information marketing is easy. Once you are able to establish a name for yourself with your information products, you just need to make sure your product's content will still be of high quality and buyers will continue to buy from you.

To make sure that your product's content will be of high quality, you must always think of your niche. Don't look at your products like how you want it to appear; look at it with how your audience will want it to appear. You must be able to find out what your niche wants to see and try to give it to them. An easy way to do that is to create a survey.

Creating a survey allows you to hear the voices of your audience and of potential buyers. You can start asking a few questions like:

- What would you expect from the product that you are going to buy?

- Do you have any challenges that you want to overcome?

- If a product being sold will show you how to overcome those challenges, would you buy it?

- What would you want to see when you buy this product?

- How much would you pay for such a product?

These will be great feedback to what you will be doing and what you will be providing in the future. One key to a successful information product is to give your audience what they want. Look into the challenges that each person may get into and give them the means to overcome them. Hearing if they want to get the item and if they are willing to pay for it is crucial and how much they are willing to pay for it.

Earning money realistically through information marketing is real. If we take e-books for example, you may earn as much as $2.00 per sale, and if you are able to sell 25 books in a month, then that gives you $50 a month. As long as you are consistent with high-quality content and are able to sell regularly, you will be able to earn more than that.

Andy Anderson

Chapter 33

Earning Money from Coaching and Keynote Speaking through Affiliate Marketing

Help always needs to be given to those in need. Such help may be physical help, or in some cases, the type of help that one will need will be with something that needs to be taught. Coaching and consulting will be the means for that kind of help to be given.

Coaching can be defined as an informal partnership between two individuals, where one is already an expert in the field and the other is still learning the processes. The person that is still learning is sometimes called the "coachee." The coach will assist the person to hit a specific goal; doing this is different from mentoring.

The word "coach" is known to have been derived from the old name of horse carriages. The word was used as a slang way back in 1830 that means the person teaching the other is being "carried" through an examination. The more popular use of the word coach is in sporting events, but it is commonly used for those who undergo adult education and personality development.

Consulting is similar to coaching in terms of giving help, but consulting leans more on giving psychological advice to a person. Being able to talk to a consultant about your issues as well as getting tips from the consultant should help you get past the issues that you are encountering.

Consulting also refers to professional help; a professional consultant is a highly trained person who will know how to approach his client with different consulting techniques. Being that he is a professional, he is trained and paid to give assistance.

Coaching and consulting are readily available for those who need professional assistance with whatever issues that needs to be addressed. This can be related to either psychological issues or personality development. With personality development, the most common topic would be financial issues. Coaching and consulting for financial issues is common, and in most cases this is what you can take advantage of. Getting help online is now the common way and being able to take advantage of that will allow you not just to help people but to earn for yourself too.

Andy Anderson

Chapter 34
Benefits of Coaching and Keynote Speaking

Coaching and consulting provide not only support but also strategies in making changes for a client. Coaches and consultants focus on what their clients need the most to solve their problems. By focusing on what the client needs the most, coaches and consultants can focus more in making the clients more successful and their goals reached.

Coaching and consulting brings a lot of benefits: It gives better perspectives for personal challenges, increases confidence, and enhances the decision-making skill.

Whether if you are a coach and consultant of a group of people in a workplace or an athletic team, there are many benefits in coaching and consulting. Not only that a coach and consultant will be offering advice, inspiration, and direction to the clients, a coach and consultant will also be motivating an individual or an entire group. Here are the benefits of being a coach and a consultant:

Delegation of building skills

One of the benefits of being a successful coach and consultant is the skill of delegating the right responsibilities and roles to the right individual. As you settle as being a coach, you will be acquiring this skill over time. A coach may be able to gain the opportunity to know the best ways to delegate, communication mediums, and additional benefits of developing closer relationships with the team members and individuals when working together in completion the assigned task.

Provides greater result

An increased greater result of team goals is one of the greater benefits of being an effective coach and consultant. When a coach motivates team members and it is highly effective and encouraging, the final result is the increased success of the team. Directing the team members how their action will greatly affect the team's goals will be beneficial not only for the team but also for the coach and consultant.

Promotes team building

When the team works together to get the goal's final result, the satisfaction felt by the coach and consultant is unexplainable and priceless. An athletic coach motivates a team to do their best whether they will lose or win. A business consultant encourages every team player to participate in their roles together to impact the company positively. A coach and consultant establish the team mentally and when the end result is a positive outcome, the coach or consultant will feel a great sense of satisfaction.

Andy Anderson

Chapter 35

When is The Best Way to Start with Coaching and Keynote Speaking?

Helping out people will give you a sense of fulfillment, but being paid to help through coaching and consultation can be better. Either you want to be a coach or a consultant; here are some steps to look at when starting:

Start making high quality contents to put yourself out.

The initial step in putting out yourself in public is by using a blog, podcast or YouTube video so that you will get found and viewed by different people. Publish high quality but free contents to attract people in viewing your articles and videos and eventually, earn constant visitors and followers. If your articles and videos are good, a lot of people will choose to work with you and hire you as their coach and consultant. Publishing books and selling information products of your own are also ways on how people can see your authority and expertise in the field and will more likely hire your services.

People would normally choose to work and hire someone who already provided them value and already established a relationship with them. So, if you have a website advertising your services as a coach or consultant, chances are, many people will not care about you since they have not heard about you or have a relationship or interaction with you before.

Once the demand is there, offer coaching and consulting services.

Once the time is there, offer your coaching and consulting services immediately. However, do not offer these services if people are not asking for it. You will know that there is demand when a number of visitors are visiting your blog or website or when a number of people are keeping in touch with you and begin asking for advice and help. When people started contacting you and seeking for your help and advice, it is a major sign that they see you as an expert and trust you as a consultant or coach to help them lift the burden or problems they are experiencing. Once the number of people gets larger, all you need to do is to set up a coaching page or an Internet page that will establish yourself as a coach or consultant.

Upon starting of your coaching and consultancy career, coach people for free to gain experience.

When it is you first time to become a coach or consultant, offer your service for free to other people to gain experience. Once you were able to get to work with a number of individuals, you will also gain some reviews and testimonials that will help you to get started with the business.

When you get enough confidence and experiences in providing coaching and consultancy services, you can begin charging small fees. As you gain more and more experience helping people address and solve their concerns, you will be more in demand and by that time, you can raise your consultancy and coaching fees a little higher than usual.

Find what your followers and viewers want and give it out to them.

Find out the main reason why people keep on visiting your blog or website and why they are asking questions and help from you: it can range from business to work related concerns, from love and dating to financial crisis. Find it out by getting at least the highest 80% questions most people are asking and begin focusing onto it. Create and center your coaching program to that specific reason.

There are generally two kinds of coaching and consultancy coaches and consultants can provide: 1-on-1 coaching and group coaching. There are still many people who cannot afford the fees for 1-on-1 coaching so they prefer to choose the later one.

Choose and screen people to know who are tire-kickers and those who are not really committed.

You have to be committed to anything you choose in order to be successful. People who are not committed are most often not successful with their goals in life since most of them are not willing to do anything. Uncommitted people wants to be successful but do not want to do any commitments to do be successful. Most are not willing to take risks or invest money and are not open to work with other people. These kinds of people always come up with several excuses and are most often, a waste of time.

Resourceful people always find several resources. If a person is really committed to do something to reach his or her goals, they are most likely willing to invest money or work extra hours every day in order to fulfill their goals. They find a way and do not necessarily make excuses.

How can you qualify and screen people? Creating an application process that they need to fill out before hiring your services is the best way to do that. This application process will help you get to know each and every one of your aspiring clients and will help you decide who you really want to work with.

Coaching and consultancy is not a passive source of income in every sense, however, it is one of the most fulfilling and rewarding thing a coach and a consultant can do. Most of the time, doing passive income sources can be considered fun and timesaving. However, doing these sources all the time will also cut your connections and relationship with all your visitors.

Coaching and consultancy are both rewarding and pleasurable especially when working with someone and assisting that person to reach his life goals. The key and satisfaction you will be getting from coaching and consultancy are incomparable with posting blog posts or YouTube videos that oftentimes, disconnects you from other people. The opportunity of having a client who you coached to be your friend is very high, since you already form a bond with them that you cannot really create or the possibility to be created through blogs and YouTube videos is very low. There are times when you will be emotionally attached to a client and at the same time, the joy and fulfillment when they achieve something is priceless. Coaching and consultancy are not only about money. It is also about the emotional fulfillment and reward you will be getting at the end.

Chapter 36
Affiliate Marketing through Video Blogging or Vlogging

Video Blogging or popularly known nowadays as Vlogging is an act of posting videos on a blog or online journal instead of the traditional pictures or themed video. It is becoming a daily habit for a lot of YouTubers or bloggers in order to keep their followers in touch with their daily lives. It is also a good way to build SEO and to increase the number of people visiting their page.

A vlog, which is also sometimes called as a video journal, is an informal video usually published on the Internet. Before Vlogging became popular, a lot of people are using different kinds of websites in order to create an online journal where different people can get to know what their favorite blogger or YouTuber is doing.

Nowadays, Vlogging is used by a lot of people as an online journal, where the owner is creating a video in order to record the things happening in his personal life. A vlog is consisted of day to day activities by the vlog owner, usually displayed in a chronological order, starting from when he or she wakes up, his or her daily activities and what is happening to his or her life up to the point when he or she is about to sleep. It can also be a combination of different pictures and videos put in together then transmitted from the vlog owner's personal computer to his or her vlog site.

Other than the individual vlog owner, multiple users can also maintain vlogs. These multiple users can create different posts about their own point of view. These multiple vloggers can be their siblings, their girlfriend or boyfriend, a close friend, a family member or a member of their organization. A lot of vlogs function not only as an online journal but also as a way to advertise the individual's hobbies, personality or even their talents. Nowadays, a lot of vloggers are using their vlogs not only to sell the products that they own but also a way for other people and companies to advertise through their videos and they will both make a profit out of it.

Chapter 37
Benefits of Keeping a Video Blog

This is now the digital age and just just snapping your fingers can easily access all information. A lot of people are now using the Internet in order to relay information and also to get the information that they need in a very quick and easy manner.

Here are some reasons why creating and keeping a video blog will help you in affiliate marketing:

Potential customers can find you fast and easy.

Every time you post a video blog in your page, it can be searched straightaway on different search engines such as Google and Yahoo. The more information and tags you put in your video blog, the more likely it will appear on top of the search engine.

It is very powerful to give your followers and potential customers a very easy way to find your page. Instead of selling your items to your prospects straightaway, which may cause them to reject your items if you force them to buy it, it will be easy if you let them find you first. Give them the liberty to look for something in you which will make them wanting for more.

A lot of your competitors may not have a Vlog Channel of their own.

Creating a vlog channel is not just sharing information about yourself as well as your day to day journey to life, it is also sharing a piece of you to your viewers. It will give you more time to share not only the products and services you are using; it also gives your customers the liberty to buy whatever you are patronizing as well. A lot of companies are doing advertisement through phone calls as well as face-to-face interactions with their prospective clients to advertise their products and service that may sound quite annoying for a lot of people. On the other hand, establishing a very strong online presence will help you not only stand out amongst the competition, it will also help you build your own list of followers.

You are building a strong relationship with your potential customers.

Creating a vlog channel is a great medium to interact not only with your existing customers but also the possible additionals. It gives your followers the opportunity to provide feedback and ask questions that is not only addressing your channel but also the things you are doing on a day-to-day basis. By communicating with them, you are building not only the trust but also the likeability of your followers to come back to you vlog channel again but also be your prospective clients in the future.

Andy Anderson

Chapter 38

Strategies in Affiliate Marketing through Your Video Blog

Build your followers listing.

By the time that you launch your video blog channel, give time to build your followers listing too. Your video blog channel will not be a profitable business if you don't have a list of subscribers and potential customers.

Tips for building your email list:

- In exchange for joining your email listing, offer some incentives like an e-book or training video, for free.

- Don't just collect email addresses; get the names of the owners too.

- Use different methods in capturing your leads. Put an option box in your blog's sidebar or generate a pop up where people may be directed to your page.

Build a lasting relationship with your subscribers.

A lot of vloggers believe that the bigger your subscriber listing is, the more money you will be able to make. This is generally true; however, your relationship with your vlog channel's subscriber listing is far more important. A good and lasting relationship with 500 subscribers is more worthy than having a bad relationship with 5,000 subscribers.

Provide your subscribers with value: know who your subscribers are, what their problems are all about and provide them all the information they need to solve those problems. One of the ways to provide consistent value to your subscribers is to send a series of email by the use of email marketing software. You may be able to send a broadcast message to your email list whenever you want, anytime you want.

Establish your credibility.

You must be separated from everyone else. Establish your credibility not only as a blogger but also as an expert in your chosen field. Have an interesting story to tell.

Chapter 39

The Best Practices When Starting with Video Blogging

One of the best sites for hosting your video blog is by the use of YouTube. YouTube is a free hosting website which is required for you to host your video blogs. YouTube gives you the capability to use the user name for your vlog account. It is also user friendly. Here are the ways on how to create your own video blog and be able to set it up in minutes.

Visiting the YouTube website.

Singing up with YouTube is easy and they offer an "Affiliate Partnership" which means that you can sign-up for a YouTube account and link it to your preferred payment method straightaway. From the moment you sign-up and started hosting your videos, YouTube will take note of all the visits and views your page is earning and there will be an equivalent amount for it.

Add your preferred user name.

You will be asked by the website to provide your preferred user name. The user name will be the URL for your video blog that people will use when visiting your video blog page. Make sure that the user name you want is available and not yet taken. Make sure as well that the user name that you will be using is easy to remember and can easily catch the attention of anyone surfing the Internet.

Enter your basic information and link it to a valid email address.

You must fill up your personal information in the form that YouTube will be providing and at the same time, you must select a valid email address that will be linked to Ad Sense and to your YouTube account. You will also enter your payment information at this point before you can proceed in setting up your actual video blog. Most video bloggers are recommending Google Mail, popularly known as Gmail for it's easy and user-friendly interface.

Setup a Password To Login

Create a password for your YouTube login so that you can have a secure account. Once you create your password, you will be asked to login again using either your username or domain name and password and you will be directed to your control panel.

Once you have set up your video blog channel, there are still a few things to remember before you publish your video blogs:

- Setup a theme for your video blog channel. Make sure it is easy to navigate. It should also be easy on the eyes as well in terms of the color scheme of your choice.

- Install plug-ins to your video blog channel. Plug-ins is another way for you to customize your video blog page. You can create a playlist for your viewers and followers so it will be easy for them to access your related videos.

- Try to install an application that will track your visitors. A recommended application will be Google Analytics.

- Start posting your content, and you can set up an "About" post to introduce yourself. The sooner you post high-quality content into your video blog page, the sooner you will be able to get visitors.

- Use easy to follow but straight to the point keywords. YouTube will allow you to link your videos using keywords. These keywords are very useful especially in search optimization. Keep in mind that the user, which is your potential follower and customer in the future, when researching, does not have any idea of what your video blog page is all about. However, if they put a keyword in the search bar that can also be found on your keyword lists, YouTube will link your page to the user immediately.

Chapter 40
Affiliate Marketing Trends

The technical changes coupled with the changes in demographics are the reasons why there is always a change in affiliate marketing. Affiliate marketing is a part of digital marketing, with the increase in the number of technological changes the field has been broadened, and because of this, there is an increasing need to adapt and discover innovative ways in which you can adapt to all the different technological changes. From the way the tracking of websites has changed to the latest developments in the cell phone industry.

As an affiliate marketer you should not just be aware of all the changes taking place in the technological dimension but also keep in sync with the continual increase of international offers and users too. As well as the tremendous increase in the usage of electronic gadgets like cell phones, tablets, laptops and so on.

With the increase in the number of users, digital marketing is the latest frontier in the field of marketing. All these factors when taken into consideration have helped change the world of digital advertising.

Let us take a look at all the different factors, which have led to the different changes in the digital market.

- **The change in models of payment.**

The basic models of payment that are being used right now are CPC, CPM, CPA and so on, these modes of payment are going to stay, but with all the advancement of technology, new methodologies for payment will become necessary. With the increase of usage of technology, the line between the real and the virtual world is blurring and there are ads and offers that are capable of serving customers on a real time basis in the real world without any geographical constraints. The technology, which is developed by Apple, the iBeacon was not delivered with this idea but it will provide the digital marketers with a whole new range of tools to facilitate their functioning.

- **Exponential growth of mobile phones**

The growth rate of mobile phones and its users is mind-boggling. And this has become a latest trend in affiliate marketing and one such trend that is bound to affect the world of marketing and technology as well. And this is the ever-increasing growth of usage of not just mobiles but tablets too. Mobile applications have even overtaken the usage of Internet on PCs these days and slowly but surely, the trend in online shopping is increasing too. Users have become open to the idea of purchasing products making use of their mobile phones and this provides a brilliant new platform for advertisers. This being said, the efforts put in by the advertisers needs to be increased for them to capture this market. The affiliates can bank in on this.

- **Cross platform growth**

The affiliate might not be able to solely rely only on the web anymore. With the increase in the users of mobile phones and tablets and also the advancement in technology, coupled with the user's willingness to make online purchases, the affiliate marketers will have to realize that they will need to not just restrict themselves to one particular platform. But will need to keep a track of offers across different platforms and devices too so that they can increase the flow of traffic to their sites. Therefore there is a growing need for the participation by experienced networks so that the task of affiliate marketing becomes simpler.

- **Increasing diversity**

The rate of diversity in established markets is increasing. The growth rate of both mobile phone and Internet users in the North American and even European markets has reached the saturation point and that being said, the existing users of technology are making use of it in different and innovative ways. The rate at which new users are being created has slowed down. People these days, for the sake of convenience, are more than willing to make online purchases. The older generations are the ones who are making use of this; therefore the marketing strategies used by the affiliates should be adjusted in a manner that would cater to this diversified group of audience.

- **International presence has increased**

Asian markets have been growing at a tremendous rate. The North American and European markets have reached their levels of web saturation, but this has opened up the doors to other international markets. The number of Internet users in China is more than 600 million. And the use of Internet is increasing at the rate of 20% per anum. This trend indicates that there is an increase in the number of international publishers, customers, advertisers and even offers. And for the affiliate marketers to stay competitive and increase their foothold, they will need to understand the way in which these new and increasing markets function. And also learn the ways in which they can create such offers that would appeal to the new customer base.

- **Content matters**

Content is important. But with the growing trend, it looks like the importance of content is ever increasing. The trend of content marketing has been increasing and this is one trend that cannot be easily dismissed. Content needs to be of high quality and it is important for not only improving the search engine rankings but also to improve the bond of trust with customers. There are millions of affiliate marketers out there, and for one such marketer to stand out they should provide the users with a reason that would want them to come back and revisit their site. For doing this, the marketers should ensure that the content they are providing is of high quality.

- **Indispensability of ad networks**

Affiliates will be able to succeed only when they find the right partnering network. In this ever changing world both in terms of demographics and technology, coupled with the invent of international users, you as an affiliate would require a right ad network to achieve success. But this not mean that it is impossible for affiliate marketers alone to go forward with their work, it just means that with the right partner they will be able to reduce their work load and overcome the challenges posed easily.

Technology has always played an indispensible role and the role it is playing will only increase in the future. It is not just the increase in the users of technology but also the changes and improvement in technology that will have an impact on the affiliate market. Affiliate marketers will have to come up with innovative an effective ways in which they cannot just retain, but also acquire new customers.

Chapter 41
Affiliate Marketing Success Stories

Do you want to build a successful website? But you know that you are no programming wizard, you don't want to invest a large portion of your hard earned money or you think that you haven't got any product to offer for sale? Well, fret not. You need not have or possess any of the above-mentioned things if you want to create a successful website.

Let us take a look at some successful affiliated sites created by individuals, and the income derived from these sites is enough to substitute their fulltime income. The key to achieving success by making use of affiliate programs is to find a particular topic that interests you, something you are passionate about. This would make your life a lot easier, because there is nothing more fun than to work on something you enjoy. Find your own niche, develop the theme of your site accordingly and ensure that you can attract as much of web traffic as possible. In this chapter we will take a look at some real life success stories about ordinary individuals who generated extraordinary results by making use of affiliate programs. About how they managed to attract a lot of web traffic and as a result ended up raking in a lot of money. When you look at all these success stories, you will notice that the true reason for their success was that they enjoyed what they were doing. Te webmasters not only had a lot of knowledge about what they chose but also were interested in doing it. Most of the traffic generated to these sites is because of word of mouth advertising and also because a lot of owners of different websites are linking their sites voluntarily out of sheer admiration for their work. Not only this, but even the search engines seem to be quite happy with providing them free web traffic, because all these sites are providing useful information that is relevant. We live in the age of technology. Where we can make use of the Internet to provide our knowledge to others living across the globe. You need not be any spectacular website to make a profit; you just need to be good at what you are doing.

Website #1

The first site we are looking at is FlickFilosopher.com. This site is an online movie review site and is operated by Maryann

Johanson. She is a movie buff and managed to turn her hobby into something that would generate a substantial income online. The way this site works is quite simple and ingenious. She writes reviews for movies and earns an income by providing the visitors with references to various DVDs, Music soundtracks and other related things. This indeed is an outstanding example of how your hobby can turn into something that helps you generate revenue for yourself.

Website#2

The second website we are going to take a look at is TvTalkShows.com. Well, this isn't a website that would blow you away with the graphics and the creative designs of the website, but then again, it must be doing something right after all, for all the traffic that it has been generating. Trevor Rieger runs this site and according to online data this site generated more traffic than the extremely popular show like jerry Springer sites. Not just this, but it has also managed to get attention from New York Times. That really is a big deal. Well, the secret of his success is quite simple actually. He built a site out of something that he enjoys doing and keeps updating it on a day-to-day basis so that his visitors don't get stale information.

Website#3

CarBuyingTips.com is the third site you should take out time and look at. This is another site that is built upon the experience of its owner. How many of you have either been the victim of a car buying scam, or know someone who was a victim of such a scam? I am pretty sure each one you must have a tale to tell about this. Jeff Ostroff the owner of this site started this website by keeping in view the way he was scammed and is now providing information so that others also don't get scammed in the manner that he was. And his website is quite helpful because it provides genuine information. Well, this might have angered quite a few car dealerships, but then again the satisfaction of helping others would trump the grumpy car dealers any day for Jeff.

Website#4

JokesaDay.com is the name of the website being operated by Ray Owens. Laughter indeed is the best medicine, and Ray Ownes seems to be making quite an effort to prove this right. This website run by him provides his visitors with jokes, puns, anecdotes and riddles. The column provided for joke of the day on his homepage is certainly bound to grab the Visitor's attention. This little idea is an innovative method employed by Ray to ensure that his visitors visit his website on a daily basis. The option of subscribing and becoming a premium member not only lets the users access all the jokes on his website for a nominal fee but is also a nice way to bring in some money.

If you want to, then you can also take a quick look at these websites to get a better idea about them. You need not have a website that is a visual treat, as long as you have got a website that provides good quality information that should do the job. You need to be able to provide the users with the information that they would require instead of prettying up the website. But if you do invest some time and money in decking up your website, it wouldn't hurt a bit. What is common amongst all the above-mentioned webmasters is that they not only know but also enjoy the subject matter they selected. The more frequently you keep updating your website, the more likely it is for the users to keep coming back to the website.

If you are looking about building a new website, it is advisable that you don't copy any of the existing sites. When you copy ideas from an existing website or even build a website similar to one that already exists, then about a month or so into it you will run out of ideas and you might not be able to update the site ever again. This happens because, the original idea was not yours, and what seemed easy initially will turn out to be quite difficult later on. So it would be better that you put in some hard work initially, and then your life would be a lot easier. You will always have more ideas when the website is your content.

One thing you will always have to keep in your mind is that, you will have to build a site that is based on a topic you are passionate about; this will help you find your niche. If you make sure that you keep updating your site regularly, content that your target audience would find useful, then even the search engines will help you by directing free traffic your way. So, all that you need to do is to find out your passion and then you can start building your site around it.

Chapter 42
Getting the Basics Right

We have covered all the important aspects related to affiliate marketing. Here is the synopsis of all the steps we have covered. This will not only refresh your memory but will also help you see if you have missed any important point. After learning and acquiring as much theoretical knowledge as possible, the only thing you will have to do after this is, take a plunge into the world of affiliated marketing. Because experience is the best teacher and only when you start working will you understand the finer technicalities of this field?

Take a look at all the articles mentioned below, this would provide you with a bird's eye view of affiliate marketing. So let us get started and summarize whatever we have covered so far.

Introduction

Have you got a website or a blog? And are looking for an option that will help you derive an earning out of your online property? Well, then you should consider making use of affiliate marketing programs available online.

Affiliate marketing is the term that has been used to portray a plan that facilitates in revenue sharing where a marketing program that is fully automated and is present online lets the webmasters place banners or advertisements of advertisers on their websites. These webmasters do so for a referral fee or a commission that they derive from the conversions that they obtain when a particular customer clicked on the affiliate link and performs the action so desired. The course of action can be a decision to make a purchase or submit newsletters to the advertiser's website or even opt in for downloads. The main reasons why advertisers invest in affiliate marketing because this not only helps in generating sales and also for lead generation.

There are various affiliate plans for you to chose from, but neither are all the plans alike nor the same returns are ensured from them. Some might provide you with the space to place an image or a hyperlink for the products; they might even allow you to put up a page for shopping or even a page that provides an inventory of all the products and content available on your website. There are other affiliate marketers who would provide you space for placing your advertisements or buttons.

Affiliate marketing jargon

There are certain affiliate marketing terms you need to be familiar with. This is essential because these terms will be used quite frequently and it will come in handy if you know what they all mean. The glossary of terms provided in this book will help you get familiarized with the affiliate marketing jargon like pay per click, pay per sale, a white list and so on.

Various affiliate programs to choose from

It is not essential that all the affiliate marketers offer the same type of programs; they will offer different programs for you to choose form. Before we get to selecting an affiliate program it is essential that you understand about the different affiliate programs that are available.

You might end up placing the hyperlinks or banners to your sites when you consider an affiliate program related to search engines and you would most likely to work on a pay per click basis. Now, those affiliates that work with email lists are those that help in promoting email newsletters. And such individuals are paid a fee when a new person opts to join the email list that has been advertised. When you are an affiliate to any merchant it means that they are going to be paid a commission depending upon the sales that take place on the website of the advertiser. Frankly speaking, of all the options available a pay per click option of payment pays the least. Because the commission is paid usually per a fixed number of clicks and usually the number of clicks is thousand. So getting paid for thousands of clicks is selling you short.

When you opt for a pay per lead option then you are provided with space for advertising your links, trial offers and also email opt in lists and so on. And the criterion for receiving payment depends upon your advertiser, you may get paid per lead that is generated or even when the user subscribes and also pays for the service obtained from the advertiser. But then again, there are chances that you receive payment or your commission for both the instances specified. From an affiliate program that is pay per sale (this is revenue sharing basis and it offers the highest commission rate) and even the amount that you are entitled to receive that is a given percentage of the total sales made. This type of an affiliate program is best suited for those sites that have a high traffic rate.

Working of affiliate marketing

It is no rocket science to understand the revenue generated by your website or acquiring knowledge about the kind of ads to be placed on it. Once you have successfully joined an affiliate program then you have the freedom to select the products or even the banners that you would want to fit into your website, and once you do this, you will receive a specific code that will help you put up these links on either a single webpage or your entire website. However, this changes when you opt for a partnership based on ad revenue. For instance let us take the example of Google AdSense, when you opt for this you will have little or in some cases absolutely no control over the manner in which advertisements are displayed in the affiliate program selected and before you go ahead with this, you will also have to agree to their agreement about the terms of service. This agreement is referred to as the affiliate agreement. And this agreement will give you all the details required to help you understand how the sales or lead generation can be tracked.

All the affiliate marketing sites provide you with the information about their site, the requirements you will have to fulfill to become an affiliate to the particular website. . Once the website accepts you as an affiliate then you will be provided with your very own affiliate ID and also the address of the webpage that will help you generate the links to be placed on your own website. You will have to choose from a host of ways in which you would want to advertise your site. When a user clicks on the link provided by your or for your website in the affiliate marketers domain, then such action of the user would be tracked by making use of the cookies generated. If the individual decides to subscribe to the marketers website then you will receive a share of the payment made by the individual depending upon the payment policy agreement.

The affiliate programs work by making use of the unique user ID provided to you and the various cookies generated to track the number of leads you have gotten and thereby the subsequent revenue generated. Most of the affiliate websites will offer a separate section on their website that will help you get your HTML code and also check information about your affiliate account. Your affiliate revenue is generated when anyone who uses your link to perform any desired action within a set time frame, such an action will contribute to your revenue.

For your better understanding, let us consider a scenario wherein an online user clocks on your link and goes through the online store attached to it, then they can be tracked by the browser cookies generated and such an individual would become your referral. There will be a time limit after which the cookie created will expire, if the individual makes a purchase before the expiration of such a cookie then you will get the referral commission you are entitled to. Now let us suppose that the user hasn't made any purchase but has created a cart of items. Even then you will get a commission provided that the cookies created haven't expired. So time is of essence in affiliate marketing. One of the major challenges you will need to overcome would be using the appropriate affiliate program that will actually help you make some money.

Some useful tips

Here are some tips that will help you get started with affiliate marketing. Always make sure that you read the fine print. The fine print is where; you will notice that all the important specifications are mentioned in. like the structure of payment, the commission rate, and any minimum amount required to be earned before a payout. Remember to compare the commissions offered by affiliate programs that are similar. Consider all the options available, but then you will have to select a few options to choose from. After you have done this, some of the criteria that will help you zero in on an affiliate program would be the merchant affiliated with the website, the website rankings and traffic, payment structure and rate and so on. Always remember that it is in your best interest to select an affiliate program that is; if not similar at least complimentary to the content of your own website. Suppose your website is all about fashion apparel then it makes sense for you to not opt for a web store that deals with home décor. It will also be helpful if the websites offer a variety of customization options for creating your own design for advertising. And lastly, do not restrict yourself to one particular type of affiliate marketing. Explore the different options available.

And also ensure that you don't believe in any of the myths about affiliate marketing. The other tips mentioned in detail in this eBook will also prove to be extremely helpful for a newbie.

Choosing an affiliate program

There are various tips you will need to keep in mind before you select a particular affiliate program. This job becomes quite difficult when there are a variety of programs to choose from. You will need to ensure that the product you are promoting or selling is something that you are comfortable with. You should have sufficient faith in the advertiser whose website you are linking yourself with. If the website seems dubious or even unreliable, then it is safe to say that even the visitors might feel the same. So steer clear of such marketers. And also ensure that the products you are selling on your website will not seem offensive to the users. It is quintessential that you select a website that offers similar services or products as your website does. Like mentioned earlier, this provides some familiarity. Putting together two different websites with entirely different content will go together as well as chalk and cheese. You do not want to put up advertisements that don't seem like they belong on a particular page. Make sure that you understand what exactly the advertiser is offering. You need to read the affiliate agreement thoroughly so that you understand what exactly is it that you are getting yourself involved in. take time to ensure that the advertiser is genuine and not a fake.

Take a look at all the various tracking tools offered for the affiliates. A genuine and a good program will be affiliate friendly and they will provide you with all the necessary tools to ensure that you can get reliable statistics of the activity going on in your site, the sales taking place and the revenue generated. There should be stylizing and various display options available to ensure that you can optimize the benefits you can derive from the advertiser's website. Another extremely important thing that you will need to consider is whether or not you are being given a good share of the revenue generated. And also go through the payment policy.

Once you have a thorough knowledge of the affiliate marketing program, then all you need to do is to take a step forward and put

Andy Anderson

all the knowledge acquired to a practical use. Yes there are certain disadvantages of affiliate marketing, but given that we live in a tech savvy age, the advantages provided by it outweigh the disadvantages. And all the success stories are bound to provide you with the required inspiration. So get your creative juices pumping and be patient. The results of your hard work will definitely pay off, maybe not immediately, but eventually.

Key Highlights

The very first take away is that, you need to understand the concept of affiliate marketing if you wish to succeed at it. Half knowledge is always dangerous and you need to amass as much information as possible in order to have a good and lasting business set up. Don't think you already have enough knowledge and try and read up as much as you can. This book has given you enough information on the topic, no doubt, but you need to read further and amass more and more information on the topic.

The next step is for you to take all the right steps towards beginning your affiliate marketing. Some people think that they should already have a popular blog if they wish to take up marketing. But that is only a misconception. You can start now and try and amass an audience in the next 6 months to 1 year. Once you have enough following, you can approach the companies to affiliate with you. For that, you will have to follow a set procedure. You cannot simply approach companies randomly and need to have a set plan in mind before you decide to approach the companies. You might get discouraged if you get rejected for not having enough traffic or being popular enough for their company to advertise with you.

It is best to start at the earliest and not waste any more time. You never know when a good client will come your way and wasting any more time will cost you. So if you have a blog, then start affiliating right away, and if you are yet to start one then start at the earliest. Once you are sorted, you can sit back and relax but until such time you will have to put in the effort to try and make the most of your writing prowess and popularity.

Once you begin, you have to have both a short term and a long-term plan for your business. Having just long term ones will not work if you don't have supplementary short term ones. You have to set 1 month, 6 months and 1-year goals for yourself on order for your business to last. Once you have started attaining the short-term goals, you need to tick them off and move to the next one. Say for example: your short term goal for the next 6 months is to try and double the number of people that visit your blog. Then, your next goal is to approach 4 companies to affiliate with you etc. The long-term goal should be to try and earn at least $350 a month.

Again, your goals should be reasonable and something that will be gettable. If you set yourself unreasonable goals then you will have a problem fulfilling them. Not fulfilling them might discourage you and cause you to take it slow. It is therefore important to set goals that are plausible. For example: planning to make $1000 from the very beginning will not be plausible. You have to set a hierarchy and then follow it accordingly.

Remember that there are several options in terms of the affiliates that you can choose for yourself. Depending on your type of blog you will have to look for the best one that suits you. If you choose something vague then it will not work in your favor. It has to be relevant to what you write about. You will find it easier to link it to your blog. I'm sure you have visited several blogs and websites where the links make no sense and you have stopped visiting them. You surely don't want that happening to you. So be careful with what you choose to affiliate with.

This point has been mentioned before and is being reiterated because of its importance. Diversification is extremely important if you wish to have a sustainable growth in terms of your affiliate marketing business. Don't stick to just one theme or topic and over the course of a year, try and diversify your topics. You need not simply expand the blogs that you have and must have two or three different ones that cater to a different topic each. If you link them together then you can pool in a large crowd.

Remember to never stop with affiliate marketing. It is one source of parallel income that is sure to bring in profits for a long time. You must not consider quitting and continue pursuing it for as long as possible. If you are finding it difficult to manage your blog alone then consider getting someone else to help out and pay him or her for their service. You can also decide to pass it on to someone you know as it is better than discontinuing it.

Lastly, make sure you take all precautionary measures to prevent getting duped by spurious websites that ask you to pay. Also make sure you check out the website you wish to affiliate with to make sure that it is to your standard.

Affiliate marketing is a great choice for you if you have a large online following. Do consider it a good option by breaking the shackles of doubt and misconceptions that enshroud it.

Conclusion

Affiliate marketing is a great way to monetize your blog and earn an online income, as well as generating passive income while you sleep or work at your day job. It is always a good idea to have a parallel source of income in order to secure your financial future.

However, it's not just a matter of signing up and getting going. You need to check out what's on offer, and be certain that you're happy to promote a particular product or service. Remember if you do it properly, affiliate marketing can take you a lot of your time, so get it right from the start.

Don't flood your website with loads of affiliate links for different products. It's likely to put the reader off because it smacks of spam. So try and limit the amount of links that you put out for your readers to go through. Use the 'soft sell' approach – create great content that your readers will keep coming back to, and gently steer them in the direction of the products and services you are marketing.

When it's done right, affiliate marketing can be both enjoyable and lucrative, but it takes time to build up online presence and trust, so don't be in too much of a hurry. Take the time to get everything right, and soon you'll be enjoying a steady stream of passive income through affiliate marketing.

If you received value from this book, then I would like to ask you for a favour. Would you be kind enough to leave a review for this book on Amazon?

Thank you so much!

CPSIA information can be obtained
at www.ICGtesting.com
Printed in the USA
LVOW10s0030240517
535560LV00016B/2104/P